BUTTE TRIVIA

GEORGE EVERETT

RIVERBEND
PUBLISHING

Published by Riverbend Publishing, Helena, Montana.

Printed in the United States of America.

3 4 5 6 7 8 9 0 MG 12 11 10 09 08

Cover design by Bob Smith
Text design by Suzan Glosser

ISBN 13: 978-1-931832-85-4
ISBN 10: 1-931832-85-4

Cataloging-in-Publication data is on file at the Library of Congress.

Riverbend Publishing
P.O. Box 5833
Helena, MT 59604
1-866-787-2363
www.riverbendpublishing.com

Contents

ACKNOWLEDGMENTS

To write this book I left my footprints on many shoulders. In many cases, by studying the work of those who have gone before, I learned amazing things I did not know about the most amazing of Montana cities. For those still among us who may have felt I was a monkey on their back while I was trying to stand on their shoulders, I apologize for all of the questions.

Thank you to Ted Duaime of the Montana Bureau of Mines and Geology on the Montana Tech campus who probably knows more about the science and history of the Berkeley Pit than anyone else. The collected works of Pat Kearney display a commanding knowledge of Butte's sports and community history.

The Butte Archives led by Ellen Crain is the Fort Knox of Butte history with maps, periodicals, books, papers, and answsers to many questions about what took place when, where, and how on this shining city on a hill since records began being kept. The major difference is that the Butte Archives allow access to the treasure of anyone who stops by and says please. A special thanks to archives staff Judy Strand for her research help.

Tracy Thornton of *The Montana Standard* has read more newspapers than anyone else and remembers a lot of what she has read. I look forward to her regular features culled from past editions called "Morgue Dust." In particular, her compilation of vaudeville performers who have visited Butte since the 1880s was invaluable. In my opinion she does not receive enough recognition for her large role in helping to preserve Butte's collective memory.

A debt is also acknowledged to researcher John Astle for his continuing excursions into the stopes and drifts of Butte history where he has plucked many fine vignettes from the yellowing pages of Butte's daily record and brought them back to life for modern audiences.

A million thanks, too, to Barbara Miller for her insights, suggestions, and comments about what is important and what is not for such a book, and for her passion for Butte's future that equals her interest in its past.

Special thanks to Janet Spencer (author of *Montana Trivia* and *Yellowstone Trivia)*, who through her careful edits showed me what a trivia book is all about. Through her diligent research and curiosity she has rightfully ascended the throne and well deserves the title of Trivia Queen.

Most of all, I give thanks each day to the spirit of Luigi, the Meaderville Maestro. May his spirit continue to haunt Butte for many years to come. Hubba Hubba.

GEOGRAPHY

Q. What was the first place name associated with the Butte area?
A. When prospectors G.O. Humphrey and William Allison "scouted for color" (went searching for gold) north out of Virginia City in 1864, they discovered gold in what they described as Baboon Gulch, now known as Butte.

Q. Where does Butte get its name?
A. The extinct volcano on the northwestern edge of the valley is still called the Big Butte. Butte is a French word for a hill that rises abruptly from the surrounding area and has sloping sides and a flat top. It is derived from the old French word *butt*, with the meaning of a mound behind a target to stop a shot.

Q. Who built the M on the Big Butte?
A. The M stands for Montana Tech (formerly the Montana School of Mines). The first three students to graduate surveyed the site. About 35 other students helped them to form the giant letter by hauling an estimated 441 tons of rhyolite, which is a form of volcanic rock.

Q. When did the M get to be so white?
A. On the first M-Day (May 20, 1910), all 50 students at the School of Mines hauled water and lime to whitewash the 75-foot wide by 91-foot long block type "M." Two years later, serifs were added to the letter, making it 90 feet wide.

Q. When were lights added to the Big M?
A. May 16, 1962. The M was outlined with 130 bulbs and on that night the switch was flipped by then Montana Governor Tim Babcock. The color of the lights can be changed for holidays like Christmas and St. Patrick's Day. And the middle lights can be alternated to reveal a flashing "V" for victory during sports events.

Q. Is Butte's elevation greater than, lesser than or equal to one mile high?
A. Greater than. Butte rests at an elevation of 5,545 ft. (1690 meters). A mile is 5,280 feet.

Q. Are Butte's deepest mine shafts greater than, lesser than, or equal to a mile?
A. The shafts, stopes and drifts of the Mountain Con underground copper mine reach one mile below the surface.

Q. What is the saying about the relationship of Butte people to their geography?
A. Butte's a Mile High, a Mile Deep, and everyone's on the level.

Q. What river system starts on the west slope of the Continental Divide and runs west to the Pacific Ocean?
A. The headwaters of the Columbia River can be found on the west slope of the Continental Divide just above Butte.

Q. How does Silver Bow County rank among Montana's counties in size—is it the largest smallest or smack in the middle?
A. Silver Bow, the county that includes the city of Butte, was once the most densely populated county in the state. It now ranks eighth.

Q. Why is the county called Silver Bow?
A. The name comes from the creek that flows through it. In the summer of 1864, four prospectors, Budd Parker, P. Allison, and Joseph and James Essler, stopped to look for gold in the creek. They stopped at a bend in the creek where the sun was shining down and the glint on the current reminded them of a curved bow of silver.

Q. In 1918, Butte was the largest city between Spokane, Chicago and Denver. What was Butte's population?
A. A check of the Butte City Directory in 1917 shows at least 91,000 residents although census numbers reflect that it never got above 65,000. Many estimates place the number at more than 100,000 living in the city at its peak.

Q. Why is there uncertainty about how many people lived in Butte?
A. At its peak, from 1917 to 1920, Butte was a chaotic city in a world at war, with people coming and going every day. Many were single miners who lived in boarding houses, sometimes sharing the same bed with a miner who worked a later or earlier shift. Many were immigrants not eager or willing to be counted by census takers.

Q. How many people live in Butte today?
A. According to 2005 census estimates, there are 32,982 residents in the combined Butte-Silver Bow County.

Q. The first concrete highway for automobiles in Montana was built near Butte in 1920. What two points did it connect?
A. The 10-mile stretch of concrete connected Anaconda to Gregson Springs (now Fairmont Hot Springs Resort). The celebration drew 10,000 people. Hundreds of cars drove from downtown Anaconda to Gregson on the new road, led by Governor Samuel V. Stewart.

Q. Butte is the only Montana city to sit at the intersection of two interstate highways. Name them.
A. The north-south Interstate Highway 15 that runs from Canada to California and 90, the nation's longest interstate that runs 3,100 miles east-west between Seattle and Boston, cross paths in Butte.

Q. I-115 is the shortest interstate highway in the U.S. federal highway system, connecting Excelsior Street on Butte's west side with the westbound I-90 highway. How long is it?
A. I-115 on the west side of Butte is all of 1.19 miles long.

Q. Who described Butte as "an island of easy money surrounded by a sea of whiskey?"
A. Butte Police Chief Jere "The Wise" Murphy who served from 1893 until his death on the job on September 19, 1935.

Q. What's the difference between a shaft and a stope?
A. A shaft is vertical and a stope is horizontal. A miner is only in a shaft to get to or come from the stope where he will work a shift.

Q. What's the difference between a stope, a drift, and a crosscut?
A. A stope is an excavation in a mine from which ore is, or has been, extracted and may or may not be used for active mining. A drift is a horizontal underground opening that follows along the length of a vein or rock formation. A crosscut crosses the rock formation – it's a horizontal opening driven from a shaft at (or near) right angles to the strike of a vein or other ore body.

Q. How many miles of stopes and drifts (horizontal) are underground in the copper mines of Butte?
A. There are about 10,000 miles of tunnels, horizontal workings, drifts, and stopes underneath the surface of Uptown Butte, which is an area of 7 square miles.

Q. How many miles of streets are in Butte?
A. 250 miles.

Q. How many miles of shafts are in the copper mines of Butte?
A. There are more than 49 miles of shafts underneath the surface of Uptown Butte.

Q. How many world-famous trout fishing rivers are within an hour's drive of Butte?
A. Five: The Big Hole, the Jefferson, the Madison, the Wise River and the Clark Fork.

Q. Where near Butte will you find the most expensive stretch of highway in Montana?
A. On Interstate 15 between Butte and Helena. A 14.4-mile stretch finished in 1986 cost about $2.6 million dollars per mile because the Boulder River needed to be redirected in rugged terrain.

Q. Where does Butte get its drinking water?
A. Drinking water for Butte is drawn from reservoirs in the

mountains and from the Big Hole River more than 25 miles south of Butte.

Q. George Grant is a famous author and conservationist who has fished Montana's rivers for trophy trout for nearly a century. What Montana river was Grant's favorite for catching lunker trout?
A. The Big Hole River southwest of Butte.

Q. How long is the Big Hole River?
A. The Big Hole flows 156 miles from its source on the east slope of the Bitterroot Mountains until it meets the Jefferson River south of Butte near Twin Bridges.

Q. Is there a hole in the Big Hole Valley?
A. Hole is an old term that was used by fur trappers to describe a valley between the mountains. Some place names remain from this time such as Jackson Hole in Wyoming and the Big Hole Valley in Montana.

Q. How many oil derricks can be found in the Butte area?
A. None. The tall black structures that dot the landscape are called headframes or gallows frames. They were used to lower miners into the underground mines and to raise up ore on the return trip to the surface.

Q. How many gallows frames can be seen today?
A. A dozen headframes remain standing on the Butte Hill since underground mining shut down, including the Orphan Girl, Travona, Anselmo, Lexington, Bell Diamond, Mountain Con, Original, Steward, Kelley (actually two side by side), and the Belmont.

Q. How tall are the gallows frames on Butte Hill?
A. They range from the Bell Diamond (99 feet tall) to the Kelley (200 feet tall).

Q. How many of the remaining headframes can be seen at night?
A. As of 2007, seven have been outlined with red light-emitting diode (LED) lights that make the structures easy to spot in the darkness.

Q. Which remaining headframe retains the most evidence of Butte's historic labor unrest?
A. The Lexington in Walkerville still holds the housing for a searchlight that scanned the surrounding terrain for snipers at night. The metal shields around the cage entryways were added to prevent strike breakers from being shot as they prepared to go down the shafts to work.

Q. How many Montana communities were established primarily to support commerce in Butte?
A. At least four: Anaconda (smelting Butte ore) Great Falls (hydropower for electricity for Butte mines) Hamilton (timber and produce) and Red Lodge (coal for Butte mines and homes).

Q. What prominent geological feature in Alberta is named after a former mayor of Butte?
A. The Frank Slide on Turtle Mountain and the nearby town of Frank, Alberta, are named for Henry Lupin Frank, mayor of Butte from 1885 to 1887, because he owned the mining property that created the town.

Q. When an earthquake hit Hebgen Lake in 1959, why were Butte miners and their heavy equipment called on to help?
A. They had the heavy equipment needed to reinforce the dam in a hurry.

Q. How far away was the 1959 quake in the Madison Valley felt?
A. Tremors from the 7.3 quake on August 17, 1959, were felt as far away as Seattle, Washington, to the west, Banff, Alberta, to the north, Dickinson, North Dakota, to the east, and Provo, Utah, to the south.

Q. How much earth was moved in the land slides triggered by the 1959 earthquake?
A. About 90 million tons.

Q. How much earth was moved to make the Berkeley Pit?
A. About 85 million tons.

Q. What is the deepest body of water in Montana?
A. The Berkeley Pit in Butte is more than 900 feet deep.

Q. The longest continuously operating seismograph in Montana can be found at the Earthquake Studies Office (ESO) in Butte. How long has it been recording seismic activity?
A. The Earthquake Studies Office (ESO) opened in June 1980 when the Montana Bureau of Mines and Geology assumed operation of the Butte seismograph station that was established in 1936 after the destructive 1935 Helena Earthquakes.

Q. What is the geological formation responsible for Butte's vast mineral wealth?
A. The Boulder batholith stretches from south of Helena to Dillon. A batholith is a geological formation caused by molten magma cooling into a large body of igneous rock, usually granite, that becomes exposed by erosion.

Q. When was the Boulder batholith formed?
A. 60 to 70 million years ago.

Q. Where is the geological formation known as The Dragonback?
A. Just East of Butte over Homestake Pass on I-90, where the Boulder batholith results in a crazy conglomeration of ruddy boulders on the east side of the pass.

Q. Where do hikers carry hammers into the hills near Butte?
A. Ringing Rocks is a strange boulder pile that attracts hikers with hammers who make "rock" music by banging on the boulders like a Flinstonian xylophone.

Q. Where else in the world can you find a similar formation?
A. The only other similar formation is in a state park in Pennsylvania where the rocks sound exactly like the music created in the hills near Butte.

Q. What was the original name for the small community of Rocker five miles downstream of Butte?
A. Foochow, so named because so many Chinese miners were working over the tailings looking for placer gold that it reminded onlookers of a large Chinese city.

Q. Because of its mineral wealth, what is Butte's traditional nickname?
A. The Richest Hill on Earth.

Q. What did Willard Scott like to call Butte on his weather broadcasts on the *Today* show?
A. He would report the weather from Tupelo, Mississippi to "2 below, Montana."

Q. When was Butte's mildest winter?
A. In 1915 the temperature never dropped below 0 degrees F.

Q. When did the temperature return to below 0?
A. In 1916 the temperature stayed below 0 for more than a month.

Q. How many other cities in the U.S. have a greater number of days when the temperature drops below freezing than Butte?
A. None: Butte has more days each year where the temperature drops below freezing (223 days) than any other city in the lower 48 states.

Q. Where do Butte's detractors say you can find the best view of the city?
A. In a rearview mirror.

Q. When did all hail break loose in Butte?
A. In 1976 a violent summer storm dropped hail the size of golf balls and caused more than $6 million in damages to Butte.

Q. How long is Butte's growing season?
A. 81 days in a normal year.

Q. What was the coldest day in Butte's history?
A. According to the National Weather Service, that day was February 9, 1933, when the temperature dropped to -52 F.

Q. What was the coldest day in Butte's history with wind chill figured in?
A. On February 2, 1989, Butte reported a wind chill reading of -91 degrees F.

Q. What was the hottest day in Butte's history?
A. The mercury reached 100 degrees F. on July 22, 1931.

Q. How much snow fell on the snowiest day in Butte's history?
A. On October 11, 1911, Butte was buried under 24 inches of snow that fell in 24 hours.

Q. How fast can the weather change in Butte?
A. On January 15, 1937, the temperature was +40 degrees F. Four days later, on January 19, the temperature was -40 degrees F.

Q. Why was a part of one of Butte's main streets, East Broadway, once known as "The Fish?"
A. East Broadway ran into the part of Butte where immigrants from Finland lived, known as Finntown. On both sides of the street you would find "Fins," so it was nicknamed the Fish.

Q. In the early days of Butte, what did it mean to be "under the clock?"
A. The city jail was in the basement of the City Hall on East Broadway and at the top of the building's tower is a large clock that is still keeping time today. Being "under the clock" meant that you were spending some time in the company and custody of Butte City's finest – in the city jail.

Q. Where did Irish immigrants settle in Butte?
A. Corktown, Dublin Gulch, and Centerville. Before the advent of automobiles and streetcars, the miners would locate their homes close to the mines where they worked.

Q. Where did the Cornish miners from the mining region of Cornwall, England, live in Butte?
A. The Cornish often lived amongst the Irish in Centerville and Dublin Gulch to be close to the mines where they worked. In the oldest areas of Butte, you can still see homes a short walk from the mine yards the Anselmo, the Mountain Con, Original, and Steward.

Q. What was the common name for a Cornish miner?
A. A Cousin Jack.

Q. What food did the Cornish bring from their native kitchens that remains a popular entrée in Butte today?
A. The Cornish pasty, a meat and potato pie wrapped in a crimped pastry shell about the size of a small football. They fit nicely into a lunch pail. When opened in the mines during lunch, they became popular among miners of all origins and were affectionately called "letters from 'ome."

Q. Where in Butte could you once find a fast-paced game of fan tan, a Pok Kop Piu lottery, a hot cup of herbal tea and a steaming bowl of chow mein?
A. Chinatown, between West Mercury, Galena, and Colorado Streets, was home to nearly 2,000 Asian immigrants until the mid-1920s.

Q. How many African Americans lived in Butte in the 1920s?
A. In a 1974 interview, Dr. Walter Duncan, an African-American podiatrist born and raised in Butte, remembered growing up with about 400 blacks in Butte in 1925.

Q. Where did most Italian immigrants live in Butte?
A. In Meaderville.

Q. Why did they call the Italian neighborhood Meaderville?
A. That area of the Butte Hill was named after an early mine developer named Charles T. Meader who owned the East and West Colusa claims long before Italian immigrants began to settle in the area that bore his name.

Q. What Butte neighborhoods were lost with the expansion of the Berkeley Pit?
A. Meaderville, Finntown, McQueen, and eventually most of East Butte, about half of the city.

Q. What is Butte's closest "suburb?"
A. Walkerville, which sits on the city's northern boundary, is a distinct and separate municipal entity with its own mayor. Walkerville is older than Butte. In Walkerville, mining began with the support of Marcus Daly and his financial backers, the Walker Brothers of Salt Lake City, to develop the Alice and Lexington Mines.

Q. What is the name of the one remaining bar in Walkerville?
A. Pisser's Palace at 301 W. Daly Street.

Q. What was the name of Butte's biggest slum?
A. The Cabbage Patch. The slum was leveled in 1940 when 225 shacks were demolished to make way for 225 new individual apartment units for low-income residents that are still operated today by the Butte Public Housing Authority.

Q. What stream that empties into the Pacific sits farther east than any other Pacific-bound stream?
A. Of all streams and rivers that flow west from the Pacific side of the Continental Divide, Silver Bow Creek rises from the most eastern point at its source on the west slope of the Continental Divide.

Q. What is the new name for Silver Bow Creek now found on many modern maps?
A. The EPA has renamed the stretch of Silver Bow Creek that flows by the Civic Center as the Metro Storm Drain or as they affectionately call it, the MSD.

Q. Where is the country's largest National Historic Landmark District?
A. Butte and Anaconda comprise the nation's largest National Historic Landmark District.

Q. Butte anchors one end of the nation's largest Superfund site. How far does it extend?
A. From Butte and Anaconda down the Clark Fork drainage to Missoula.

Q. How much copper was removed from the Berkeley Pit?
A. About one billion tons of material has been removed from the Berkeley Pit since 1955. Within the first year of operation, the pit extracted 17,000 tons of ore per day, much of it averaging only 0.75 percent copper or about 127 tons of copper.

Q. How much mineral wealth remains in the water in the Berkeley Pit?
A. According to Fritz Daily, the value of minerals contained in The Pit's water has been calculated to be approximately $500 million in 1999 and up to $800 million in 2020.

Q. How much has been spent on environmental reclamation in the Butte area?
A. More than $100 million dollars has been spent over the last 20 years to address the consequences of more than a century of hard rock mining and smelting.

Q. Where was Bell Creek?
A. On the Flat below the Northern Pacific Depot and beyond Silver Bow Creek. Three miles long and deep enough for diving, it was the most popular swimming hole in the summer for the children of Butte for many years.

Q. Where did the name for the Travona mine come from?
A. Most likely, the original owner William Farlin, a native of Cornwall on the southwest tip of England, named it after a beautiful stretch of coast there named Trevone.

Q. Where did the phrase "Butte, America" come from?
A. Often used to describe the unique and separate qualities of Butte compared to the surrounding state of Montana and the rest of the world, the phrase was conceived by college students in Missoula as an insult and embraced by Butte residents as an apt description of their locale. Shag Miller, former station owner and broadcaster for KBOW, started promoting the concept on the radio and distributed bumper stickers that read "Butte, America." A polka was suggested as its new national anthem.

Q. How many "Butte, America" bumper stickers did Miller and KBOW give away?
A. 15,000.

Q. What do you call a native of Butte?
A. Buttians, Butte Rats, or Beauts, but if you call them Butt-ocks you better be prepared to back that up with more than a smile.

Q. What is a bohunk?

A. This derogatory term for an immigrant from Eastern Europe was embraced and turned into a long standing traditional annual celebration at Butte High School that included costumes and parades. It was called Bohunkus Day.

Q. How many mountain ranges are visible from Butte?

A. Four. The Highlands (south), Pintlars (southwest), Flint Range (northwest) and the East Ridge (the Continental Divide) to the east.

Q. Where was Highland City?

A. Located in the hills south of Butte, Highland City was a busy mining camp with ten stores, three saloons, two dance halls, two lodge halls, restaurants, and rooming houses. By 1921 Johnny Kern was the last resident. Like most boom camps, when the claims stopped paying out most boomers moved on to the next prospect or gave up and took a job in Butte.

Q. Where is Timber Butte?

A. Timber Butte is the butte at the south end of Summit Valley that is covered with – timber. The most prominent feature on Timber Butte is the large zinc ore bin left over from a zinc processing plant that was owned by W.A. Clark. It now serves as a private residence with a solar greenhouse, a design studio for the artists and designer who live there with a great view of Butte. The unique home has been featured in several magazine articles and was the subject of a 2003 episode of HGTV's *Extreme Homes*.

Q. Where did the Berkeley Pit get its name?

A. The Berkeley Mine was an underground mine in Meaderville. That neighborhood and the mine were both consumed by the expansion of the open pit mining operation that bears its name.

Q. Where is Elk Park?

A. Elk Park is located about ten miles north of Butte. A park is a natural plateau between high mountains formed by an ancient streambed.

Q. What happened to the lake that used to grace the valley floor below Butte?
A. Lake Avoca was a large lake on the valley floor in Butte's early days. It was a rural part of the city that would attract visitors for canoe rides and picnics. As more people moved onto the Flats and the city grew, the lake was drained to make room for new homes and streets and businesses.

Q. Is Butte sinking or rising?
A. Relative to the East Ridge, Butte is sinking along the Continental fault line about 1 to 3 millimeters each year based on tests in 1906 that were confirmed by reevaluation in the 1970s.

Q. How much have the Flats sunk since the valley was first settled?
A. About 1 foot.

Q. Why is Butte sinking?
A. Geologist David Alt says that one theory is that the Continental fault is simply slipping, but there is no sign of slippage where roads cross the fault. Most likely, the fault is stuck and the earth's crust is bending, accumulating energy like a drawn bow. If this is the case then the fault will eventually slip and release the accumulated energy in an earthquake.

Q. Are there many earthquakes around Butte?
A. Montana is one of the most seismically active states in the country, and the most active area of Montana is the southwest part of the state which includes Butte. Major earthquakes have been experienced within 200 miles of Butte in 1869, 1872, 1897, 1925, 1935, 1947, 1959 (the largest on record) and 2005. Helena's most devastating quake was 6.5 in 1935 – knocking down 900 buildings. The 1995 quake in Kobe, Japan, was 7.2 and killed 6,000.

Q. What caused a tsunami in the Berkeley Pit in September 1998?
A. About 1.3 million cubic yards of "loose" alluvium on the southeast wall sloughed into the pit's lake. This caused a three-foot rise in the water level and surface waves greater than 20 feet.

Q. What is a gulch?
A. A gulch is a deep V-shaped valley formed by erosion that usually contains a small stream or dry creek bed. Butte is surrounded by place names that refer to these narrow valleys. Brown's Gulch, Sheep Gulch, Hail Columbia Gulch, Meadow Gulch, Buffalo Gulch, Missoula Gulch, Dublin Gulch, French Gulch and German Gulch are some of them.

Q. Where was Dogtown?
A. Dogtown was a neighborhood in Butte's southwest area also known as Williamsburg after the manager of the Colorado Smelter there, Henry Williams. Along with the smelter, the area also included two breweries, the Centennial and the Tivoli, that employed mostly German immigrants.

Q. Who lived in the Boulevard neighborhood of Butte?
A. Immigrants from Croatia dominated the Boulevard neighborhood in the area south of Front Street on Montana Street. The streets there were lively in February with the pre-Lenten public celebration of Mesopust, a festival of spring renewal similar to Mardi Gras and Chinese New Year. Croatian immigrants also get credit for bringing along the recipe for one of Butte's most enduring treats - *povitica*, a nut roll dessert of yeast bread similar to a strudel with one or more fillings, usually walnuts. It is traditionally made to celebrate special events and holidays, especially Christmas.

Q. The Beef Trail Ski Area built in 1938 southwest of Butte was one of the first downhill ski areas developed in Montana. Why is it called The Beef Trail?
A. In the late 1860s, as soon as gold mining became established in Montana, the livestock industry was established to raise cattle and sheep to feed and clothe the miners of Butte. Cattle were driven to Butte through this area from ranches to the south and the west to a packing house near what is now Stodden Park.

Q. Did they butcher the cattle in Butchertown?
A. No. The neighborhood just north of Walkerville just beyond the Alice Pit bears the name of Rollo Butcher, the original owner of the Alice Mine, who sold his claim to the agent of the Walker Brothers, Marcus Daly.

Q. Where did the wood come from for Butte's mines and homes?
A. One place was Woodville at the south end of Elk Park above Butte at the top of what is known as Woodville Hill. The name comes from the camps for woodcutters, mostly French Canadian, who worked and lived there.

Q. Where can you find The Drives?
A. The Drives is the neighborhood close to St. Ann's Catholic Church near Harrison Avenue on The Flats. Its name comes from the number of streets that are named drives such as North Drive, Cross Drive, Center Drive, South Drive, West Drive and East Drive. The area was once the location for Butte's circus grounds.

Q. When was the first street paved with asphalt in Butte?
A. Wyoming Street was paved with asphalt in 1938.

Q. Where did the Spanish-speaking residents of Butte worship?
A. The second Sacred Heart Church at 448 E. Park Street was rededicated on November 27, 1913, after the first was destroyed in an electrical fire a year earlier. The church was designed in the California mission style with a bell to call the faithful to worship. Hundreds of Hispanic families came to Butte for work, many from the Southwest at the invitation of William Andrews Clark who had mining interests in Arizona, Nevada, and Utah. The second Sacred Heart was lost to the expansion of the Berkeley Pit.

Q. Why are there so many places named for parrots in Butte?
A. The abundance of Parrot in Butte place names—Parrot Lode, Parrot Mine, Ramsdell's Parrot, Colusa Parrot, the Parrot Smelter, and Parrot Flat—are all related to a popular attorney named R.R. Parrot who helped claim developers with critical financial and legal advice.

Q. Where was Parrot Flat?
A. The area of Butte's East Side below the Belmont Mine was named Parrot Flat, where mostly Croatian immigrants lived. The neighborhood was named after the smelter that was previously located there which, in turn, was named for the early Butte

settler R.R. Parrot. While the development of the Berkeley Pit didn't directly gobble up Parrot Flat, many residents moved away rather then endure daily explosions in the nearby open pit mine.

Q. Where could you find tropical trees in Butte at one time?
A. Until the late 1980s, the Capri Motel on North Wyoming Street planted a live palm tree in its center court to confuse and amuse its guests.

Q. Where was the Smokehouse Lode?
A. One of the finest restaurants in Uptown Butte, the Acoma, sits on the site of the Smokehouse Mine at 65 E. Broadway. Originally there was a small cigar shop called The Smokehouse. When the owner decided to build a hotel and excavation started, copper was discovered. Instead of a hotel, the Smokehouse Lode produced several million dollars worth of ore. When the mining was completed, the Acoma Hotel was built on the spot. It is no longer a hotel, but it is one of the city's finest restaurants after a major renovation in the mid-1990s.

Q. What caused the biggest flood in Butte's recorded history?
A. On June 4, 1908, more than 9 inches of snow fell and quickly melted, making streets impassable and swelling an already over-flowing Silver Bow Creek to nearly a mile wide. Every bridge between Butte and Anaconda as well as railroad tracks were washed out.

Q. What was memorable about Memorial Day in Butte in 1927?
A. It was not a good day for a picnic. On May 29, 1927, Butte residents woke up to find that more than 22 inches of heavy spring snow had fallen during the night, interrupting phones, streetcars, and electric service to the city.

Q. What was the cause of Butte's 1943 flood?
A. On March 28, 1943, rising temperatures caused heavy mountain snows to rapidly melt, sending spring floods rushing down Silver Bow Creek and washing out bridges, roads, and railroad tracks in its path downstream.

Q. What is the name of the neighborhood that borders Missoula Gulch?

A. McGlone Heights is a Butte neighborhood of modest homes built in the 1950s to house families displaced by the expansion of the Berkeley Pit. It is located on either side of North Excelsior Street just below Walkerville on Butte's Upper West Side. The neighborhood is named after the Anaconda Company's then Vice President of Western Operations, Edward S. McGlone.

Q. Why does a tunnel from the Lexington Mine in Walkerville exit in Butte by the Syndicate Pit?

A. The Lexington Mine, which put A.J. Davis on the road to becoming Montana's first millionaire, was a great producer of gold and silver in Walkerville. When the owners realized that the taxes in Walkerville were higher than in Butte, they dug a tunnel down the Hill to take out the ore in Butte, where the tax bite would be less painful.

Q. Where did many early mine workers remain out of sight and out of mind when off shift?

A. A small community of several streets north of Walkerville housed miners for the Alice, Moulton, and Lexington Mines. The residents, mostly Cornish, lived close to their places of employment but far enough away from other parts of Butte and the rest of Walkerville that the neighborhood became known as "Seldom Seen."

Q. Why is Butte's large municipal park named Stodden Park?

A. It's named after Thomas Stodden, Mayor of Butte City from 1919 to 1921.

Q. There is a large timbered park on the south edge of the Summit Valley called Thompson Park. Who is it named for?

A. It is named in memory of William Thompson, Mayor of Butte City from 1895-1897. However, the creation of the park is the work of his son, William Boyce Thompson, a millionaire who made a fortune in the copper industry and donated the land for the park between Blacktail Creek and Roosevelt Drive in 1917. In 1922, the municipal park on the edge of wilderness was expanded with help of the federal government with a memorandum of understanding between the U.S. Department of

Agriculture and the Mayor of Butte City, the only agreement of its kind in the United States before or after.

Q. Why is the state highway through the mountains from Butte to Whitehall called The Harding Way?

A. The name of the stretch of highway was announced as a gift to President Warren G. Harding on his visit to Butte on June 29, 1923. He was presented with a photograph of the stretch of highway that snakes up to Pipestone Pass. The photograph was given in a frame of pure copper poured in Anaconda that weighed 97 pounds.

SCIENCE AND
NATURE

Q. What is the Berkeley Pit?
A. One of Butte's (and the country's) most dramatic geographic features, the Berkeley Pit is the result of one of the world's largest truck-operated open pit mines. It was opened in 1955 and operated until 1982.

Q. Why is the Berkeley Pit full of water?
A. Underground pumps operated around the clock to keep water out of underground mines. ARCO bought the mining properties from the Anaconda Company in 1977 and decided to turn off the pumps in 1982. The underground mines quickly filled with water and the Berkeley Pit has been filling ever since. It was a "watershed" event – underground mining would never be possible underneath Butte again. An era had ended and the event led to a long period of mourning in the Mining City.

Q. How much water is in the Berkeley Pit?
A. About 36 billion gallons.

Q. How big is the Berkeley Pit?
A. The Berkeley Pit has an area of about 675 acres. It stretches 1.5 miles from east to west and about 1 mile from north to south.

Q. How deep is the Berkeley Pit?
A. From bottom to surface, the Berkeley Pit is about 900 feet deep according to the Montana Bureau of Mines and Geology that monitors the area. The water level was 5,261.81 feet above sea level in October 2006, up from 5,128.86 feet in October 1996.

Q. What's the water like in the Berkeley Pit?
A. The water in the Berkeley Pit is highly acidic with high concentrations of arsenic, copper, cadmium, cobalt, iron, manganese, zinc, and sulfate. The deep water of the pit lake is separated from the shallow water by a zone of rapid chemical and physical change between 35 to 50 feet below the surface. The pH of the water closest to the surface is 2.5, about as acidic as soda pop.

Q. When will the Berkeley Pit overflow?
A. According to Pit expert Ted Duaime, the Pit will not overflow because federal orders have established the maximum level that the water will be allowed to reach - 5,410' above sea level. Failure to keep the water below this level would result in steep fines (up to $7,500 per day). The rim of the Berkeley, even at its lowest point, is at 5,509' - almost 100 feet above that critical water level. Even if the water level were allowed to rise unchecked, the water would still never overtop the pit's rim. At some point, instead of flowing toward the Pit, as it does now, the water would begin to flow away into the void spaces between the sand grains in the alluvial aquifer. This underground water movement would prevent the Pit water from ever approaching the rim.

Q. How will the water in the Berkeley Pit be treated?
A. The Horseshoe Bend Water Treatment facility came on line in November 2003 to begin removing metals from about 2 million gallons of water a day from the Yankee Doodle Tailings Pond. The treated water is routed for use in the milling operations at Montana Resources and no water is discharged into Silver Bow Creek. A 4-inch sludge discharge pipeline runs whatever is not used in the milling back into the Berkeley Pit.

Q. How much did the Horseshoe Bend Water Treatment Facility cost to build?
A. $18 million.

Q. When will the Horseshoe Bend water treatment plant be used to treat the Berkeley Pit water?
A. The EPA Record of Decision for the Berkeley Pit requires that the treatment plant must be ready to treat at least 7 million

gallons per day at least two years before the water in the Pit approaches 5,410 feet above sea level.

Q. When is the Berkeley Pit expected to reach the critical action level of 5,410 feet above sea level?
A. 2020.

Q. What Butte woman has a fungus named for her?
A. In 1992 Andrea and Don Stierle, cancer researchers and "bioprospectors" from Butte's Montana Tech, found a previously unknown fungus that produces a cancer-killing substance in bark from a yew tree in Glacier National Park. In honor of Andrea, they named the new organism *Taxomyces andreanae*.

Q. How many different bacteria and fungi have the Stierles been studying?
A. Since 1996 Andrea and Don Stierle and their assistants have isolated and studied more than 50 varieties of bacteria and fungi, including one which shows promise to prevent migraine headaches and another that precipitates heavy metals from Berkeley Pit water.

Q. What previous research with fungus in Butte has resulted in an organic pesticide that is an effective weapon against grasshoppers, white flies and other agricultural pests?
A. The Mycotech Corporation developed a patented mycoinsecticide containing spores of the bug-killing fungus *Beauveria bassiana* for use in organic agriculture.

Q. How many migrating snow geese died after they stopped to rest on the surface of the Berkeley Pit in 1995?
A. 342.

Q. How many snow geese migrate by Butte each year?
A. About 300,000.

Q. How many snow geese have died in Butte since 1995?
A. None. Ever since the tragedy of 1995, the Berkeley Pit has been equipped with noise nuisance that is activated during migrations to discourage "pit stops" by migrating fowl.

Q. How many elk range less than 20 miles from Butte's city llimits?
A. About 2,000 elk live in the Mt. Haggin Wildlife Management area near Fleecer Mountain about 15 miles southwest of Butte.

Q. Where is the last place in Montana to find the river-dwelling artic grayling, a rare and endangered fish?
A. The last native population of arctic grayling can be found in Montana's last best river, the Big Hole River about 20 miles south of Butte.

Q. Why are artic grayling endangered?
A. The only populations of arctic grayling native to the lower 48 states were in Michigan and Montana, and the Michigan population is now extinct. The arctic grayling was once wide-spread throughout the upper Missouri river drainage as far downstream as Great Falls. Lewis and Clark made note of these "new kind of white or silvery trout" in 1805. Today the only known location where they remain in Montana is the Big Hole River with the largest concentrations found near Wisdom, Montana.

Q. The first settlers came to Butte looking for gold and then silver. Did they find much?
A. From 1880 to 2000, the Butte Hill mines have produced 2,922,446 ounces of gold and 725,486,448 ounces of silver.

Q. How many different minerals have been found underneath Butte's surface?
A. 130. These include copper sulfides and sulfosalts like bornite, chalcocite, colusite, covellite, digenite, djurleite, enargite, pyrite, barite, quartz, rhodochrosite, silver, and many others.

Q. How many pounds of copper were taken from Butte between 1880 and 2000?
A. 22,799,000,000 pounds.

Q. If that copper was used to pave a highway from Butte, how far would it reach?
A. According to the Montana Bureau of Mines and Geology located

on the campus of Montana Tech in Butte, that much copper could pave a four-lane highway four inches thick from Butte to 30 miles south of Salt Lake City, which is 450 miles south of Butte.

Q. So, has mining in Butte been worth it?
A. The total value of mining production in Butte is equivalent to $48 billion in today's dollars with half of that coming from copper.

Q. What's the most valuable metal ever mined in Butte?
A. Copper is still king in terms of quantity mined, but molybdenum or "Moly" is a metal that is used to harden steel and is often found along with copper. It sells for more than ten times the amount of copper. Between 1880 and 2000, Butte mines produced 326,671,890 pounds of molybdenum.

Q. After copper, what other ores were almost as plentiful between 1880 and 2000?
A. 4,909,202,540 pounds of zinc, 3,702,787,341 pounds of manganese and 854,797,405 pounds of lead were also taken from Butte during this time.

Q. During the same time, how much sulfuric acid was a byproduct of copper mining and smelting operations?
A. 9,456,105 dry short tons.

Q. How many pounds of waste rock were removed to produce each pound of ore?
A. The rule of thumb is three pounds of overburden or waste rock for every pound of ore.

Q. How much can the mining haul trucks at Montana Resources, the company that operates the active copper mine in Butte, carry in each load?
A. Older trucks are smaller and they can only load 170 tons. Newer trucks can carry 240 tons per load.

Q. How much did the newer, larger trucks cost?
A. $2.2 million – each.

Q. How tall are their tires?
A. 14 feet tall.

Q. What was the most common form of death among Butte miners?
A. Although accidents happened in the mines, killing about one miner a week between 1914 and 1920, the more common killer was silicosis, more often called miner's con, caused by inhaling rock dust over an extended period that scarred lung tissue.

Q. How prevalent was silicosis among Butte miners?
A. In a federal health study in 1916, of 1,018 Butte miners tested, 42 percent had silicosis.

Q. What was the position of the Anaconda Company when confronted with the problem?
A. They produced their own scientific study that pinpointed the cause of silicosis as the unsanitary living conditions of Butte miners in their own homes.

Q. In Butte, what is a Grizzly?
A. In most of Montana, the answer would be a large bear of the species *Ursus arctos*. In Butte, it is a mining term that refers to a coarse screen used to remove oversize pieces from blasted rock.

Q. Why is copper considered a strategic metal?
A. Since just before World War I, every bullet and every artillery shell uses a copper casing (or brass which contains even more copper). Copper-jacketed bullets and shells allow for much higher muzzle velocities than the lead used previously because copper has a much higher melting point, greater specific heat capacity, and is harder. Copper is also needed to make guns themselves and copper is used extensively in the assembly of airplanes and ships and for various wiring needed to conduct electricity.

Q. Is copper still used to make U.S. pennies?
A. Before 1982, all U.S. pennies were made of 95 percent copper and 5 percent zinc. Since 1982, pennies have been made with

97.6 percent zinc, with 2.4 percent being a thin copper coating, or "clad."

Q. Where did the idea to use something other than copper for pennies come from?
A. U.S. pennies were first made from zinc in 1943 when a serious copper shortage during World War II required an alternative. That year, pennies were made from steel with a covering of zinc. The copper saved by making pennies out of steel (rather than copper) was estimated to have allowed the military to meet the combined copper needs of "two cruisers, two destroyers, 1,242 flying fortresses, 120 field guns and 120 howitzers" or enough for 1.25 million shells for artillery guns.

Q. What disease commonly linked to raw eggs was named after a Butte doctor?
A. Salmonella was named after Dr. Daniel E. Salmon who discovered and studied the disease while managing a hog cholera research company in Butte until he died there in 1914.

Q. How many residents of Silver Bow County died from the global Spanish Influenza outbreak of 1918?
A. 640. At the same time, 316 young men from Silver Bow County were killed during World War I, according to the Butte Archives.

Q. Who was Montana's first pathologist?
A. Dr. Caroline McGill started working in Butte's Murray Hospital as a pathologist on January 1, 1911.

Q. When did Dr. Caroline McGill gain the right to vote?
A. Three years later in 1914 along with other women in Montana and Nevada.

Q. Which Butte doctor started one of Montana's most prestigious museums?
A. Dr. Caroline McGill's lifelong collection became the nucleus for the Museum of the Rockies in Bozeman. She lived and worked in Butte until her retirement in 1956 when she packed up all of her collections and retired to her beloved 320 Ranch in the Gallatin Valley.

Q. What is Butte's official flower?
A. The rare *Clarkia pulchella*, commonly called pink fairies, an herb in the Evening Primrose family, was reintroduced and cultivated by Master Gardener and Urban Forester Norm DeNeal in Butte at the Lexington Mill Gardens on the corner of Granite and Arizona streets.

Q. How much did Archie Rice of Walton, New York, win in 1924 for proposing and erroneously answering the question "In what American city is there no living green things and why?"
A. Rice received $5 from *Liberty Magazine* for his question and wrong answer "Butte, Montana, because of the sulphur dioxide fumes from the smelters" even though open air smelting had ended in Butte by 1910.

Q. How many gardens did Alma Higgins visit when she counted Butte gardens in 1920?
A. 80.

Q. What group did Alma Higgins found in Butte in 1922?
A. Higgins helped form the Rocky Mountain Garden Club.

Q. How many members did the club have by 1928?
A. 400. The main gardening club in Butte today is the Butte Garden Study Group with a very active membership of 60 gardeners.

Q. Who is responsible for establishing National Garden Week?
A. National Garden Week, celebrated throughout the country, was started by Alma Higgins of Butte. Today, the National Council of State Garden Clubs continues to observe National Garden Week during the first week of June.

Q. What was the nickname given to Alma Higgins?
A. The Christmas Tree Lady. She started a campaign to encourage Americans to decorate living Christmas trees. As a result of her efforts, a living Christmas tree was planted and decorated on the White House lawn in 1924.

Q. Why do so many rose bushes bloom in Butte in June?
A. In 1927 and 1928, the Rocky Mountain Garden Club worked with the Butte public schools to encourage rose cultivation in Butte and purchased rose bushes for 25 cents each.

Q. How many rose bushes were planted by school children in 1927 and 1928?
A. 1,500 in 1927; 2,500 in 1928.

Q. How many new trees have been planted by volunteers in Uptown Butte?
A. From 2003-2007, volunteers in Butte led by the Madrazo family have planted nearly 500 Canada red chokecherry, crabapple, patmore ash and mountain ash trees on Butte's city streets.

Q. Who served as the President of the National Garden Clubs from 1957 to 1959?
A. Evelyn Mooney of Butte.

Q. How did a soldier who served in the army of "the Desert Fox" during World War II come to be one of Butte's most renowned gardeners?
A. Erich Loch served in the German army under General Erwin Rommel in North Africa until his capture in 1941. He was sent to a prison camp in Lethbridge, Alberta. After the war, he moved to Butte where a relative was living. He lived in Butte the rest of his life until his death in 2003 at the age of 81, becoming an expert at growing plants of all kinds in the harsh climate, especially poppies, which he grew to crowd out weeds.

Q. How long did a dog named The Auditor live on the shores of the Berkeley Pit?
A. The Auditor was first spotted roaming the mine in 1986 and continued to haunt the diggings for nearly 20 years. Mineworkers named him The Auditor because he would disappear for days on end and then show up when he was least expected.

Q. What breed of dog was The Auditor?
A. A Puli, which looks much like a shaggy sheep dog.

Q. Has Butte ever had a beloved canine mascot before?
A. Dynamite was a collie-shepherd cross that lived at the intersection Park and Main Streets during the 1910s when he wasn't hopping a streetcar to Clark's Park or Columbia Gardens. The story is that Dynamite loved anyone in a uniform. One day he hopped a streetcar carrying the Boston and Montana Band to the train station for a trip to Los Angeles. Dynamite joined them on the train trip to Southern California and never returned to Butte.

Q. What is the nickname of bornite which was mined in Butte?
A. Bornite is commonly known as *"peacock ore"* because when exposed to the air the mineral forms an iridescent tarnish made of assorted copper oxides or hydroxides that form a very thin layer. When light waves bounce between the bornite surface and the top of this layer, they leave with the wavelengths of various colors. This effect is the same as the rainbow effect that occurs on the iridescent neck feathers of a peacock or pheasant. In the case of bornite, the tarnish will have a purplish, violet or blue color.

Q. Where besides Butte will you find abundant deposits of Covellite?
A. Bor, Serbia. Covellite, an indigo blue copper sulfite was first identified in Mount Vesuvius by Italian mineralogist Nicolo Covelli (1790-1829) and has been found in abundance under Butte's surface, most famously in the Leonard Mine. Today it gives a name to a popular summer theatre at 215 Broadway, the Covellite Theatre, home of the Buttenik Ensemble.

Q. What unusual location did two retired miners choose for a garden?
A. In 1986, in a nod to adaptive reuse, two former miners were arrested for growing marijuana in the defunct Paraiso gold mine near Elk Park. Police hauled away 305 mature plants under cultivation in the mine.

Q. What animals lived and worked alongside the miners in Butte's underground mines?
A. Mules shared the work with men in Butte's underground mines. In 1910, there were 1,000 mules underground in the mines.

Q. How many mules were used to provide horsepower in Butte's mines?
A. 10,000 mules worked underground in Butte's mines over 30 years.

Q. What was the motto of Butte's first union?
A. "A man is worth more than a mule."

Q. What replaced mules in the mines?
A. With the advent of abundant electrical power, by 1923 all mules but two were replaced with 200 four-ton locomotives.

Q. Where did electricity for Butte mines come from?
A. Hydroelectric power generated at the Great Falls of the Missouri River.

Q. How did the electricity get to Butte from the dams at Great Falls?
A. It was transmitted to Butte on a 100,000-volt power line.

Q. What is Butte's most noxious weed?
A. While spotted knapweed is a close second, *kochia scoparia*, commonly called kochia, can grow up to 6 to 8 feet tall if untended in Butte weed lots.

Q. Which one of Butte's most popular restaurants was named for a beaver?
A. Chequamegon is an Algonquin name for beaver. Many Butte residents found the name for the highly popular restaurant at 27 N. Main Street too hard to pronounce and they simply called it the "Chew and Be Gone." Today the same address is the location of the popular Columbian Garden Espresso which dedicates part of its wall to a menu from the Chequamegon.

Q. Where can you see a house bloom in Butte?
A. Usually during the first week of June, if you drive west on Platinum Street from Montana to Excelsior, you'll notice a house in bloom with pink blossoms. About 50 years ago, the owner trained a crabapple tree (not vines) to grow on the walls using a technique perfected in Europe known as *espalier* that flattens and attaches the tree limbs to the masonry using small nails and straps.

Q. What were the scientific effects of arsenic in Butte's air from heap roasting in the 1880s, according to William Andrews Clark?
A. Clark declared in a speech that arsenic was a disinfectant that killed microbes and a mild cosmetic that gave Butte women their beautiful pale complexions.

Q. What were other reported effects of exposure to arsenic and sulfur from heap roasting?
A. Policemen who were exposed to the open air for extended shifts complained of stomachaches, and the smelter smoke was attributed as the cause for nosebleeds and nausea. From July to October 1890, Butte recorded 192 deaths and many could be linked to reactions to the smoke. In December 1890, smelter smoke covered the city 28 times, and 36 deaths were caused by breathing-related diseases.

Q. How much sulfur was in the air from the smoke of heap roasting in the 1890s?
A. Every 24 hours, according to contemporary measurements, 260 to 300 tons of sulfur were released into the Butte air.

Q. When did open roasting of ore end in Butte?
A. By 1910, because of the consolidation of mining properties under one company, most of the mines on the Butte Hill sent their ore to Anaconda or Great Falls for smelting.

Q. What was the physics that made the Granite Mountain-Speculator Fire Disaster of 1917 so deadly?
A. At the time the two mines were probably the best ventilated mines on the Butte Hill. The Granite Mountain had a powerful downdraft while the Speculator mine had an equally powerful updraft allowing air to move at 200 to 300 feet per minute. When the fire began in the Granite Mountain Mine these forces contributed to spreading deadly smoke throughout the diggings, resulting in the death of 168 miners.

Q. What is the recommended action level for cleanup of arsenic in soil in Tacoma, Washington, a city with an industrial environment similar to Butte?
A. 100 parts per million.

Q. What is the recommended action level for cleanup of arsenic in soil in Butte, Montana?
A. 250 parts per million (ppm) for residential soil, 500 ppm for commercial soil and 1,000 ppm for recreational land.

Q. What is the recommended action level for cleanup of lead in the soil in the nearby state of Washington?
A. 250 parts per million.

Q. What is the recommended action level for cleanup of lead in the soil in Butte, Montana?
A. 1,200 parts per million (ppm) for residential soil, and 2,300 ppm for non-residential soil.

Q. What is a vug?
A. A vug is a term introduced by Cornish miners to describe small cavities in rock formations that are created when crystals form and are later eroded away, leaving behind voids. Fine crystals and geodes are often found in the open space of vugs.

Q. What Butte-based housing organization has had a national impact on how homes are built throughout the country?
A. The National Affordable Housing Network (www.nahn.com), founded by Bob Corbett and Barbara Miller of Butte, is a national organization that has developed house plans incorporating resource-efficient building science of super insulation with heat recovery ventilation. Homes from these plans have been built in Montana and across the country. Their plans, which demonstrate how to build affordable homes that use resource-efficient technologies to reduce water and energy usage, are often used by Habitat for Humanity affiliates. In 2006, the Network was recognized by the Alliance to Save Energy with their prestigious national Andromeda Award.

Q. How many brain surgeons have come from Butte?
A. At least two, both from the Sorini family. Ernest Sorini of Butte practices medicine in Michigan. Peter Sorini, his younger brother, lives and works in Butte. In 2006 when ABC News anchor Bob Woodruff sustained head wounds from a blast in Iraq he was operated on in Landstuhl Germany by Lt. Col. Dr. Peter Sorini of Butte who was on active duty there.

Q. How many stuffed African elephants are there in Butte?
A. Only one. Atcheson Taxidermy is a family business that has been practicing the taxidermic arts in Butte since 1951 for a wide range of wild animals taken by hunters around the world, and if you bring an elephant to them they will stuff it for a fair price.

Q. Can you arrange an African safari in Butte?
A. The Atcheson family in Butte will get on the phone to their friends in Namibia and arrange one for you. They have been arranging hunts around the world since the first hunt was organized by Jack Atcheson, Sr., in 1955.

Q. How many species of trout can you catch on the Big Hole River south of Butte?
A. Five: German brown, rainbow, brook, cutthroat and the last fluvial (river-dwelling) grayling trout in the Lower 48 states.

Q. What is a joint tree?
A. In the Boulder Batholith above Butte, tall pine trees grow between boulders. The trees take root in crevices where the wind blows soil and seeds into the fissures (called joints). In this way huge pine trees flourish in inhospitable rock crevices. Along with wind, rain, and ice, tree growth is a natural force that wears down rock to elemental gravel and  soil. Trees grow until they split the boulder crevice that nurtures them. When the wind topples the trees and they rot away, there remains no trace of what split the boulder.

Q. Why are many of the trees turning a rusty red color in the mountains around Butte?
A. The mountain pine beetle has invaded and killed these trees. The U.S. Forest Service estimates that an estimated half-million acres of lodgepole and ponderosa pine are under attack by mountain pine beetles (*Dendroctonus ponderosae*) in Montana.

Q. What did Butte native William Boyce Thompson decide to do after he made a fortune in the copper mining industry?
A. After visiting Russia during the revolution and seeing widespread starvation, Thompson decided to do something on his

return to America. In 1920, he established an institute for plant research in New York. Thompson expected the institute to make valuable contributions to general scientific knowledge, to biology, and to medicine. The Butte native named the institute in honor of his parents, Anne Boyce Thompson and William Thompson (the mayor of Butte City from 1895-1897), and endowed it with $10 million.

Q. Does the Institute exisit today?
A. Yes. Founded in Yonkers, New York, the institute relocated to Cornell University in 1978 and continues its work today. For more information, see http://bti.cornell.edu/.

Q. How much "seed money" did Thompson donate to establish the Boyce Thompson Institute for Plant Research?
A. $10 million dollars.

Q. Did the Boyce Thompson Institute live up to its two founders expectations?
A. Since its establishment in Yonkers, the Boyce Thompson Institute has made fundamental discoveries in the fields of plant biology, agriculture, environmental sciences and human health. Among many plant biology discoveries, the Institute developed a rooting hormone now used extensively in the nursery industry to propagate plants quickly and efficiently. The hormone is a stable derivative of a natural hormone called indole acetic acid.

Q. What have they achieved in agricultural research?
A. In agricultural research, they discovered the biological and chemical basis for selectivity in herbicides and developed the first herbicide that could control specific weeds without harming other plants.

Q. What is the track record of the Boyce Thompson Institute in environmental research?
A. They developed the first computer models for testing the combined effect of ozone and acid rain on mature forests.

Q. What results has the scientific research of the Boyce Thompson Institute achieved in the areas of human health?
A. In the process of studying how to stabilize dry, stored seeds, they discovered a new technology for stabilizing insulin to allow it to be delivered to diabetics through an inhalable dry aerosol spray instead of by injection. They also discovered that vaccines against diseases can be delivered orally through food. They have developed modified plants that deliver "edible vaccines" against human diseases, including hepatitis B.

Q. Who from Butte is responsible for nurturing a better understanding of desert plants in the Arizona desert?
A. Northeast of Tucson and east of Phoenix in Superior, Arizona, is the Boyce Thompson Arboretum with the mission to instill in people an appreciation of plants through the fostering of educational, recreational, research, and conservation opportunities associated with arid-land plants. The Arboretum was established with an endowment from Butte native William Boyce Thompson.

Q. What Native American tribes claimed the area that would become Butte long before gold was discovered there by white prospectors?
A. Evidence of temporary encampments as long ago as 12,000 years has been found that point to the presence of Salish, Shoshoni, Nez Perce and Bannack people visiting the area to gather plants or hunt buffalo and other big game.

Q. What plants did native people dig for and gather in the valley below Butte?
A. Camas root, bitterroot, biscuitroot, and breadroot.

Q. Why weren't there more permanent settlements in the area?
A. Winters were brutal and the area was vulnerable to attacks by raiding parties of the Blackfeet and Crow. After hunting and gathering, the local tribes would retreat to the relative safety of the Bitterroot Valley or beyond.

Q. When Edgar S. Paxson moved to Butte to work as a theater set painter for John Maguire, where was his favorite place to hunt for antelope?
A. On the plateau that is now the campus of Montana Tech.

Q. Where did pioneer Granville Stuart report abundant big game including a large herd of buffalo?
A. In the valley below what would become the city of Butte.

Q. When was the last time the natives dined on buffalo in Butte?
A. They still do today. Butte has businesses that pack and ship buffalo steaks and burger around the country. One company makes spaghetti sauce with buffalo meat and you can pick up buffalo sausage at Duane's Sausage and Specialties on North Main Street.

Q. What is one of the most frequently sighted birds in Butte?
A. Throughout Butte, especially in winter, one of the most frequent encounters is with *Corvus corax*, the raven, defending a perch on a headframe, pondering how to retrieve something from the rim of a dumpster, or fighting over a french fry with another raven in a parking lot.

Q. Where is one of the best places to observe the *aurora borealis* on a winter night, according to locals in Butte?
A. Near Moulton Reservoir above Walkerville.

Q. Along Harding Way by Thompson Park there are two well tended crosses on the side of the road by Blacktail Creek. What do they represent?
A. They memorialize a tragic automobile accident that took the life of a man and a moose. One is for the man, the other is for the moose.

Q. Where are you most likely to see a moose in Butte?
A. While they often wander into residential neighborhoods of The Flat, moose are more often seen eating willows along the creek beside Harding Way.

Q. What is there to watch for in the large meadow at the intersection of Montana Route 2 and Continental Drive at the south end of the Summit Valley?
A. In wet springs, the large meadow blooms with *Dodecatheon clevelandii* or pink shooting stars.

Q. Are there rats in Butte?
A. Although a Butte resident is a self-pro-
claimed Butte Rat, and a popular newspaper
column is titled the Rat Chat, there are no rats
of the *Rattus norvegicus* or other varieties that
live in Butte.

Q. Can you see hummingbirds in Butte?
A. Yes. Throughout the city in the summer if you hang a feeder,
you will see hummingbirds of the Rufous and Calliope tribe stop
by for a drink.

Q. What Montana city counted the most *Bombycilla cedrorum*
or cedar waxwings in the 1999 Audobon Society Great Backyard
Bird count?
A. 200 were counted in Butte, the most of any location in Montana that year. These birds are famous in Butte for eating fer-
mented berries and bouncing off windows in a drunken stupor.

Q. What bird is a sure harbinger of spring on the Butte Hill?
A. Although robins are seen in spring, the sure sign that warmer
days are ahead is the sighting of *Sialia currucoides*, the beautiful mountain bluebird.

Q. Does Butte enjoy a butterfly bloom?
A. Lilacs thrive in Butte and they bloom relatively late, at-
tracting migrating Tiger swallowtail (*Papilio glaucas)* butter-
flies which in some years fill the streets of Uptown Butte as
they flit around the tall buildings looking for food.

Q. Where's the best place to get a fishing hook in your ear
near Butte?
A. During late May and mid June, depending on water flow and
temperature, if you hazard the banks of the Big Hole River you
will encounter the annual bloom of salmon flies that hatch on
the river, spurring a feeding frenzy among the river's trout. A
more dangerous frenzy occurs among fly fishermen slapping the
river surface in front of them, the bushes behind them, and the
fishermen beside them with their fly lines.

Q. How fast does the salmon fly hatch travel along the Big Hole River?

A. The salmon fly hatch moves along the river about three to five miles a day. Throughout the summer, the Big Hole River experiences hatches of caddis, stoneflies, midges and mayflies, among others, and the variety of insects challenges the skills of fly fishermen to match the latest hatch with artificial flies.

HISTORY

Q. What was the first job held by Butte pioneer Marcus Daly?
A. Before coming to work in the Comstock Lode in Virginia City, Nevada, Marcus Daly started out tending pigs in his home village of Ballyjamesduff in Cavan County, Ireland. In 1855 he emigrated to America at the age of fifteen. He learned about hard rock mining on the Comstock Lode before coming to Butte as an agent of the Walker Brothers to inspect and purchase mining properties.

Q. What year was the first recorded instance of mining in the Butte area?
A. In 1856 Caleb E. Irvine passed through the valley and reported that someone, most likely a Native American, had tried to dig a pit using elk horns. That was the source for the name of the mine that was developed on that  site — the Original. The Original mine went on to produce millions of dollars of ore from the time it was developed in 1878 until it was closed in 1940, reaching a depth of 3,569 feet below the surface.

Q. Who was Montana's first millionaire?
A. Andrew Jackson Davis of Butte. In 1868 Davis started out on his road to riches by acquiring a group of mines and a small quartz mill for $20 and a horse. Davis expanded the stamp mill and began concentrating his efforts on silver. When Davis couldn't turn a profit on silver mining, he lost his silver holdings to the bank. Ironically, A. J. Davis went on to have a lucrative career in banking, founding the First National Bank and becoming Montana's first millionaire. Other successful ventures included copper mines, flour mills, and livestock.

Q. Where did the name Anaconda come from for the mine and the company?
A. Michael Hickey, the original owner of the claim, remembered

an editorial by Horace Greeley that he read as a Union soldier during the Civil War. Greeley described how the Army of the Potomac would surround and squeeze to death the Confederate Army like a giant Anaconda.

Q. How much did Marcus Daly pay Michael Hickey for the Anaconda mine?
A. Daly bought the Anaconda Mine in 1876, the same year as Alexander Graham Bell invented the telephone, for $30,000 in partnership with George Hearst and Ben Ali Haggin, his California investors.

Q. When the Nez Perce War broke out in 1877, who led a group of volunteers from Butte to track them down?
A. "Captain" William A. Clark.

Q. When was the first union formed in Butte?
A. On June 13, 1878, the Butte Workingman's Union was formed.

Q. How many members did the Butte Workingman's Union start with?
A. 261 members.

Q. Who was the first Mayor of the city of Butte?
A. Henry Jacobs, a German Jewish clothing merchant and former vigilante, was elected on April 15, 1879.

Q. How many eligible voters cast a ballot in that election?
A. 123 of the 2,500 eligible chose to exercise their right to vote and elected Jacobs by a vote of 72-51.

Q. What was the first local ordinance passed into law by the new city of Butte?
A. After a large fire burned many wooden buildings, Butte's first law required new buildings to be built of brick instead of wood.

Q. When did Butte get electricity?
A. In 1880, shortly after Walkerville was wired, Butte street lights were powered by electricity — eight years before Montana became a state and two years before New York City was electrified.

Q. Which Earp brother served as a Butte policeman *before* the shootout at the OK Corral?
A. Morgan Earp was a Butte policeman from December 16, 1879, to March 10, 1880. He joined his brothers in Tombstone, Arizona in time to get shot in the shoulder during the shootout at the OK Corral on October 26, 1881.

Morgan was ambushed the next March and mortally wounded while playing billiards with his brother Wyatt. Wyatt set out to avenge his brother on a three-week Earp Vendetta Ride in the country surrounding Tombstone, killing anyone related to the Clancy clan who he held responsible for his brother's murder. Morgan was laid to rest on family property in Colton, California dressed in a blue suit provided by his friend Doc Holliday.

Q. How many rooms does William Andrews Clark's Butte home, The Copper King Mansion (www.thecopperkingmansion.com), which was built between 1884 and 1888, have?
A. 34.

Q. How much did Clark's Butte home cost to build?
A. $240,000. If the mansion was built today it would cost $5,191,416.

Q. How many rooms did William Andrews Clark's New York City mansion on Fifth Avenue have?
A. 131.

Q. How much did Clark's New York mansion cost to build?
A. $3,000,000. If built today, Clark's New York mansion would cost $65,596,529. The mansion was demolished in 1928.

Q. Which Butte business is the oldest owned by the same family in Montana?
A. Whitehead's Cutlery at 71 E. Park Street in Butte is run by Donna Whitehead, the descendant of founder Joseph Whitehead who established the business in 1890.

Q. How many family owned and operated businesses in Butte were established more than 50 years ago and are still operating today?
A. At least nine: Miller's Shoes (founded after the Granite Mountain Mine Disaster in 1917), Rudolph's Standard Furniture (founded by German Jewish immigrants in 1919), Wein's Men's Store (founded by German Jewish immigrants in 1906), Pekin Noodle Parlor (founded by a Chinese immigrant family from Canton in 1909), Thomas Family Clothing (founded by Lebanese immigrants in 1902), Whitehead's Cutlery (founded in 1890), Richard & Rochelle's Men's Store (founded by a Russian Jewish immigrant as Spier's in 1915), Steele's Warehouse (founded in 1934) and Town Pump (founded by the Kenneally family in 1953).

Q. Callahan the Bum, a famous character who roamed Butte's streets in the 1890s and 1900s, once passed out on the street in front of a saloon. When pranksters from the bar rubbed limburger cheese on his moustache while he was unconscious, what did he say when he woke up?
A. "Damn, boys, the whole world stinks."

Q. What ever happened to Lizzie Borden's maid Bridget Sullivan after she testified at Borden's trail for the notorious axe murder of her parents in Fall River, Massachusetts, in 1893?
A. After the acquittal of Lizzie Borden, Bridget returned to her native Ireland but soon returned to America and moved to Anaconda, Montana. She died in Butte in 1948.

Q. How did Chinese entrepreneurs respond to a boycott of their Butte businesses?
A. In the winter of 1896-1897, union members blocked doorways and discouraged customers from entering Chinese restaurants and laundries. A group of Butte Chinese businessmen fought back. They protested to the governments of China and the United States and then filed a lawsuit against the leaders of the boycotts. They won their claim to damages of lost business in the amount of $500,000.

Q. How much did the Chinese businesses collect from their judgment?
A. They were only able to collect $1,750.05 to cover their legal fees and expenses.

Q. How much money was gathered in Butte for an ambulance corp during the Boer War in South Africa in 1899?
A. $10,000. That amount would be equivalent in purchasing power to $250,746.27 in 2006 dollars.

Q. Where did several soldiers return to work after their service in the Boer War?
A. Several Irish veterans were employed in the Butte mines after serving on the side of the Dutch against the British in 1899.

Q. In 1900, when the U.S. Senate declared the election of William Andrews Clark void due to blatant bribery in the Montana state legislature and forced him to resign, who was appointed to replace him?
A. William Andrews Clark. Clark conspired with his ally Lt. Governor A. E. Spriggs to lure the Governor Robert B. Smith to California on business. Then as Acting Governor, Spriggs appointed Clark as his own successor.

Q. How many union members were in Butte by 1900?
A. By 1900, 34 different unions advocated for nearly 18,000 Butte workers in a variety of trades. Unions represented the construction trades, brewers, teamsters, blacksmiths, and hackmen. Musicians had a Protective Union as did Theatrical Stage Employees and Theatrical Ushers. Teachers had the Butte Teachers Union. Other unions represented typographers, waitresses, and bartenders. Even newsboys had their own union and their own strikes.

Q. When did the railroad arrive in Butte?
A. On December 21, 1881, the Utah & Northern line arrived in Butte connecting the city to Ogden, Utah. Five days later, the first passenger train arrived in Butte.

Q. How many railroad lines eventually served Butte?
A. Five. The Utah & Northern arrived first (1881), followed by the Montana Central (1883) which later became part of the Northern Pacific, then the Great Northern (1889), the Butte, Anaconda and Pacific (1893) and the Chicago, Milwaukee, St. Paul & Pacific (1908). The Northern Pacific reached Butte from the East in 1890.

Q. What did most of the trains carry?
A. In 1910, the city received 16,000 freight cars a month and handled 17,280,000 tons of freight. Most of that was ore from Butte's mines.

Q. How many passenger trains arrived in Butte daily at the railroad's peak?
A. According to Thornton Waite, author of *Union Pacific, Montana Division*, 38 passenger trains brought passengers to and from the city each day on the five railroads serving Butte by 1917.

Q. How many passengers came and went to Anaconda on the Butte, Anaconda & Pacific Railroad?
A. Before the advent of roads, automobiles, and busses, four trains hauled about 1,000 passengers a day.

Q. What tragedy wiped out Butte's first fire department?
A. On January 15, 1895, the fire department responded to the Kenyon Connell warehouse fire where, unknown to them, 350 boxes of dynamite were illegally stored. In the explosion that followed, all but three of the fire department were killed. Many others died as two more explosions killed would-be rescuers and spectators. In all, three explosions killed 57 people, including the policeman who first called in the fire.

Q. Where will you find the capstan, the vertical rotating cylinder used to hoist and lower the anchor, of the *U.S.S. Maine* that was sunk in Havana harbor in February 1898, precipitating the Spanish-American War?
A. Near the entrance of the Butte-Silver Bow Courthouse at 155 W. Granite Street.

Q. How many gardeners were employed planting flowers at Columbia Gardens, the famous Butte amusement park, in 1899?
A. A crew of 15 full-time employees worked to plant a variety of more than 150,000 flowers in 1899.

Q. How much did it cost to take the trolley to Columbia Gardens on every summer Thursday, known at the Gardens as Children's Day?
A. It was free.

Q. How many watermelons were given away on Commercial Day August 21, 1907, at Columbia Gardens?
A. 10,000.

Q. What did all kids drink for free every Miner's Union Day (June 13) at Columbia Gardens?
A. Ice cold lemonade.

Q. When did the Montana School of Mines (to become Montana Tech) first open?
A. 1900.

Q. How many students were in the first class?
A. 21.

Q. What was the tuition for each student in 1900?
A. Montana residents paid $5; out of state or foreign students had to pay an additional $25.

Q. What foreign language was one of the most frequently heard on the streets of Butte in 1900?
A. There were 12,000 Irish immigrants in a population of 47,635. Walking on the streets of Butte at that time, you would have been more likely to hear Gaelic rather than English. Some mines even posted their job openings in Gaelic.

Q. How many Irish immigrants returned to Ireland to buy a farm?
A. According to researcher Riobard O'Dwyer, only 124 Irish immigrants of the thousands who came to Butte ever returned to buy land and live in Ireland.

Q. What Native American tribes called Butte home around 1900?
A. Bands of the Chippewa and Cree tribes lived on the outskirts of Butte. They came to Montana from Canada in the late 19th century seeking the remnants of buffalo herds and roamed the state until they were granted a small reservation in 1916 near Havre called Rocky Boy's, a bungled translation of the chief's name, Stone Child.

Q. What U.S. Senator held interests in Butte's red light district?
A. Lee Mantle, publisher of the *Daily Inter Mountain* newspaper, mayor of Butte and U.S. Senator, was the legal owner of record of the Blue Range and adjacent "cribs" in what was Butte's red light district in 1900.

Q. When did telephone service come to Butte?
A. The first union local of telephone operators in the country formed in Butte in 1902.

Q. Why was F. Augustus Heinze called a "courthouse miner?"
A. Heinze, one of the fabled Copper Kings, used the 1872 Mining Act to his advantage and bribed judges to increase his fortunes. He owned mining properties but he accrued a fortune through favorable judgments in Butte courts.

Q. What was the Apex Law?
A. This theory, which was incorporated into the 1872 Mining Act, stated that whoever owned the apex or closest place that an ore vein came to the surface owned the entire vein of ore. Heinze used this aspect of the law to his great benefit by stating that wherever he mined, he was only pursuing a vein that "apexed" on his property.

Q. Once the lawyers got involved, how did Heinze ensure that suits would be settled in his favor?
A. Through staunch loyalty to his interests and many say through bribery, Heinze had the solid support of District Judge William Clancy who presided over many of the cases brought to settle these apex disputes. Clancy had a long flowing beard that would often contain evidence of recent meals. Contemporary accounts report that he would nod off during a complex argument in his court only to be stirred in time to pronounce "I rule for Mr. Heinze!"

Q. When did frustration with Heinze and Judge Clancy cause the layoffs of 20,000 Montana workers?
A. On October 22, 1903, before unemployment insurance, Amalgamated Copper Company in Butte put 20,000 Montanans out of work until the Montana legislature agreed to meet to pass a change-of-venue law. The event was known as The Great Shutdown. After

a special session of the state legislature was called to pass a change-of-venue law in December, mining in Butte resumed.

Q. Why did Omaha detectives Henry Dunn and Henry Feltfedt travel to Butte in October 1905?

A. After nearly five years as a fugitive, Omaha kidnapper Pat Crowe was arrested in Butte's red light district for the sensational December 18, 1900, kidnapping of Eddie Cudahy, heir to an Omaha meatpacking fortune. Cudahy's son was returned unharmed shortly after his father paid his ransom. After Crowe's capture in Butte he was returned to Omaha and tried but public sentiment ran strong against the excesses of the meatpacking industry and Crowe was seen as a Robin Hood character. He was acquitted and moved to New York City after being released.

Q. What is one of the most unique causes of death on Butte death certificates?

A. In 1906, at least five certificates described the cause of death as suicide by dynamite.

Q. What was the cause of several accidental deaths in Butte around the 4th of July?

A. Underestimating the safe distance from exploding dynamite sticks.

Q. How many Sullivans lived in Butte in 1908?

A. In 1908 there were 1,200 Sullivans living in Butte from as many as 77 different families in County Cork, Ireland. Today you can still find about 100 listings for Sullivans in the Butte phone book.

Q. Who did prominent Butte Chinese businessman Hum Fay wed in 1909?

A. An American-born socialite from Spokane's Chinese community named Chew Gum.

Q. Who interrupted Carrie Nation's temperance crusade through Butte's Venus Alley in 1910?
A. On January 25, 1910, Madam Mae Meloy of the Irish World tussled with the famous temperance crusader and saloon smasher. One account says that Meloy shoved her down a flight of stairs but more likely she mussed her headgear and hair as she jostled Nation toward the exit and invited her to abbreviate her visit to the brothel. Carrie Nation retired after her Butte visit.

Q. How many "soiled doves" were counted in Butte in 1910?
A. According to Montana historian Ellen Baumler, in 1910 there were more than 250 working girls in Butte.

Q. What did Rose Herron sell and where did she sell it?
A. Rose Herron was known as Shoestring Annie. She moved to Butte from Colorado about 1910 and after her husband died she took to selling shoestrings to survive. Her sales pitch consisted of perching by the miners' pay office with a cigar box full of laces and as miners flush with their pay envelopes would try to walk by she'd yell out "Buy a pair of shoelaces you goddamned cheapskate!"

Q. In 1912 Montana Power Company was formed from how many electrical companies serving Montana customers?
A. 40. These small providers merged into four regional companies that were consolidated into Montana Power which was formed in Butte under the leadership of John D. Ryan.

Q. When the Butte Silver Bow Courthouse was completed in 1912, what was one of its first uses?
A. It served as barracks for state militia sent to Butte to impose martial law during the labor unrest of 1914.

Q. How many second-class passengers on the *Titanic* were heading to Butte when it sank on April 15, 1912?
A. William Gilbert was working in Butte when he decided to return to his native Cornwall to visit his family. He was traveling in second class under ticket number 30769. Frederick William Pengelly was a 19-year-old from Southhampton returning to work in the Butte mines with the ticket number 28665. Neither was ever found.

Q. What relative of Butte millionaire William A. Clark was last seen on the first class deck of the *Titanic*?
A. A nephew of Senator William Andrews Clark, Walter Clark, who lived in Los Angeles, was among the first-class passengers on deck who went down with the ship. His wife survived.

Q. At what Butte grocery store did the idea of self-serve grocery shopping begin?
A. The Lutey Brothers in Butte pioneered the concept of self-service grocery stores at 146 W. Park Street and at several other store locations in Butte, allowing customers to put their own groceries in self-serve baskets. William Lutey received approval to patent the words "Marketeria and Groceteria" on May 27, 1913.

Q. What was the cause of Lutey's closing?
A. During World War I Lutey became an outspoken advocate for federal food policy to support the war and sold English goods in his store. Both positions were unpopular among Butte's Irish. When supporters of the Irish Free State asked for a donation, the Luteys refused and the Irish called for a boycott. The final blow came when copper prices spiraled down after the war. The last Lutey's store closed in Butte in 1924.

Q. What was the requested donation that the Irish Free State supporters were refused that prompted the crippling boycott?
A. $150.

Q. What grocery store chain took the idea of self service and made it its own?
A. Clarence Saunders of Memphis, Tennessee, visited Lutey's in 1914 or 1915 before starting the Piggly Wiggly grocery chain that popularized the idea throughout the South.

Q. How many Chinese-owned businesses operated in Butte in 1914?
A. 62. Today, there remains one still operated by the same family that established the business - The Pekin Noodle Parlor at 117 South Main Street.

Q. During the labor unrest of 1914 in Butte, what happened to the Miner's Union Hall?
A. Dynamite blasts demolished the building on June 23, 1914, to finish the destruction begun during a riot on June 13th.

Q. How many blasts did it take to demolish the Miners' Union Hall?
A. Witnesses counted 25 blasts during the night.

Q. What happened to the first Miner's Union Hall?
A. It collapsed during construction in February 1882.

Q. How much had the union spent building the hall before it fell down the first time?
A. $23,000.

Q. Which Butte mayor shot one of his constituents to death?
A. Lewis Duncan. On July 3, 1914 a drunken Finnish miner, Erick Lantilla, upset that the mayor was not doing enough for the Finns and the I.W.W., stabbed the mayor in his office. In self-defense, Duncan shot him.

Q. Which political party did Duncan belong to?
A. Duncan was elected mayor of Butte on the Socialist ticket in 1911.

Q. How many electric customers did Montana Power Co. have in 1915?
A. 32,000. The company's annual revenues were $4.3 million.

Q. After he was murdered on August 1, 1917, where was Industrial Workers of the World (I.W.W.) labor organizer Frank Little buried?
A. In Butte's Mountain View Cemetery.

Q. When Frank Little was murdered he had a note pinned to his clothes that read 3-7-77. What did that mean?
A. No one knows for sure but one theory is that it refers to the dimensions of a grave - 3 feet wide by 7 feet deep by 77 inches long.

Q. Where was the worst hard-rock mining disaster in U.S. history?
A. The Granite Mountain-Speculator Mine Disaster in Butte in 1917.

Q. How many miners died during that tragedy?
A. 168.

Q. How many miners usually died in the underground mines of Butte on average per week?
A. One

Q. How many automobile dealerships did Butte boast in 1918?
A. 28. Today, there are about a dozen.

Q. What famous American military leader was stationed in Butte during World War I?
A. Captain Omar Bradley was a young officer stationed in the West when most of his peers were being sent to fight in Europe. While they fought in France, Bradley would enforce public order in Butte and organize baseball games for his troops. His time would come later, however, when, as a four-star General, he would help plan and execute the Allied invasion of Germany that ended World War II.

Q. Who was the first casualty after the arrival of Bradley and his troops?
A. Bradley's pregnant wife fell ill when they arrived in March 1918. While she recuperated, his son was stillborn in Butte.

Q. Where did several Butte recruits serve during World War I?
A. In 1918 federal troops were called to Butte, Anaconda and Great Falls to quell labor unrest. After being sent for basic training at Fort Lewis, Washington, instead of going on to France, Butte recruits were sent to Butte for guard duty during labor unrest against their civilian neighbors in their own hometown.

Q. Did these troops from Butte see action in Butte?
A. They were called out to restore order and police the streets during the 1918 St. Patrick's Day celebration which turned into a riot.

Q. Who did President Woodrow Wilson appoint as Deputy Secretary of War in 1918?
A. John D. Ryan of the Anaconda Company in Butte was placed in charge of the Bureau of Aircraft Production (BAP). Four days later, the U.S. Army Air Service was created and took over responsibility for administration, training, aircraft requirements, personnel, and facilities from the Division of Military Aeronautics. On August 28, 1918, Woodrow Wilson appointed Ryan as a Second Assistant Secretary of War and civilian Director of Air Service, the precursor to the U.S. Air Force.

Q. What New York property was the Finlen Hotel modeled after?
A. The Hotel Astor in New York City. Originally, the Finlen Hotel was designed to have two towers like the Astor but because the bottom fell out of the copper market as it was being built in 1922, the top of the second tower was never built.

Q. How long was Butte occupied by troops?
A. Butte was first occupied by state militia in 1914 when the dynamiting of the Miners Union Hall during an internal union dispute gave the Governor a pretext to remove Butte's elected Socialist mayor and sheriff from office. U.S. Army soldiers returned and stayed for the better part of four years, first in August 1917 after the Granite Mountain Disaster precipitated a violent strike, then again in 1918, again in 1919, and again in 1920 after the deadly incident known as Anaconda Road Massacre. Troops were finally withdrawn from Butte in January 1921 shortly before mining was suspended in April due to falling prices and a growing stockpile of copper during a post-war downturn. When mining resumed in January 1922, it was also the end of Butte's primary importance to the Anaconda Company. In 1923, the company purchased mining properties in Chile where eventually two thirds of its profits would come from.

Q. What was the size of William A. Clark's estate at his death in 1925 at the age of 86?
A. $200 million.

Q. How much would that be worth today?
A. About $2,000,000,000 dollars.

Q. Where else did nationally renowned architect Cass Gilbert design a classic Beaux Arts style building besides the Metals Bank & Trust in Butte?
A. The Supreme Court building in Washington, DC.

Q. Butte has the state's longest running "Buy Local" campaign. When was it started?
A. On January 18, 1926, The "Buy in Butte" Bureau formed and established headquarters on the 6th floor of the Metals Bank.

Q. Which store boasted the first escalator in Montana?
A. Burr's Department Store at 66 W. Park St. in Butte.

Q. How many Butte businesses featured live monkeys in their display windows?
A. Two—rival shoe stores The Shoetorium on West Park Street and Newman's Bootery on East Park Street.

Q. What U.S. ambassador to the Irish Free State came from Butte?
A. W.W. McDowell of Butte who also served the shortest time of any ambassador to Ireland. His appointment was made on January 15, 1934. He presented his credentials on March 27, 1934, and then died at his post less than two weeks later on April 9, 1934.

Q. Where in Butte did former U.S. Senate Majority leader and U.S. Ambassador to Japan Mike Mansfield meet his wife Maureen?
A. Senator Mike Mansfield first spotted his lifelong love Maureen while walking to work past her home on Washington Street in 1928. He worked as a miner from 1922 to 1931.

Q. In what branch of the service did Mike Mansfield serve - Navy, Army or Marines?
A. All three.

Q. Who was the first president of the Montana Federation of Negro Women's Clubs?
A. When the Montana Federation of Negro Women's Clubs first met in Butte on August 3, 1921, at least nine black women's clubs were active in Montana communities throughout the state. Representatives from seven of the local clubs attended the meeting to organize the state federation as an affiliate of the National Association of Colored Women's Clubs, which organized in 1896. The representatives attending the Butte meeting elected Mary B. Chappell of Butte as the state federation's first president.

Q. What was Mary B. Chappell's Butte women's' organization called?
A. Chappell led the Pearl Club, established in 1918.

Q. Why is Clark County, Nevada, named after William A. Clark?
A. Clark County, the Nevada county that contains the city of Las Vegas, is named for William A. Clark, the mining and railroad magnate who first owned the land the city was built upon. Clark bought the land in 1902 from Helen Stewart to serve as a roundhouse location for his Nevada trains and crews.

Q. How many churches served the spiritual needs of the faithful in Butte in 1917?
A. 47 houses of worship served Butte for a variety of faiths. Today there are 35 churches to serve the spiritual needs of residents and visitors.

Q. How many saloons did Butte need to quench the thirst of a wide-open town in 1917?
A. 250 saloons operated in Butte then. Today, there are about 50 watering holes in Butte.

Q. During Prohibition how many of these were closed?
A. In 1923, most of these were still in business with the same owners at the same location, having changed their names to soft drink parlors or cigar stores.

Q. During Prohibition in 1923, how many new soft drink parlors opened in Butte?
A. 44.

Q. What has been the largest religious faith practiced in Butte?
A. Roman Catholicism.

Q. How many parishes did Butte once have?
A. Ten. Today, Butte still has six parishes that are part of the Helena Diocese.

Q. How many Catholic churches and schools did Butte once have?
A. In the 1950s there were at least 10 Catholic churches and nine Catholic grade schools. These were Sacred Heart, St. Patrick, St. Ann's, St. Lawrence O'Toole, St. Mary's, Immaculate Conception, St. John's, and St. Joseph's. Two more churches in Meaderville shared one grade school.

Q. What did Catholic miners call waste rock from the underground mines?
A. "Protestant ore."

Q. How many synagogues served Butte's Jewish community?
A. Two.

Q. How many remain?
A. One remains—the B'Nai Israel Synagogue on the northeast corner of Galena and Washington Streets with an active congregation.

Q. What congregation in Butte celebrates Christmas in January?
A. The Serbian Orthodox Church on Continental Drive serves the spiritual needs of immigrants from Eastern Europe and they celebrate Christmas on January 7th.

Q. From what country did many Protestant immigrants to Butte come?
A. China. Many Chinese immigrants fled China to avoid persecution for their Christian beliefs. A Chinese Baptist Mission on West Mercury Street helped many to learn English and assimilate into society after their arrival in Butte.

Q. Who was Butte's most famous pickpocket?
A. Jew Jess was arrested and brought before a judge who was forced to dismiss charges against her for lack of evidence. Elated, Jess embraced the judge who shortly after discovered that his watch, wallet, tie pin, and lodge emblem had disappeared.

Q. What former Montana governor is buried in Arlington National Cemetery?
A. John Woodrow Bonner, Governor of Montana from 1949 to 1953, who was born in Butte on July 16, 1902. In 1940 he resigned from his position of Attorney General to join the Army and rose to the rank of Colonel before he was discharged in 1946. When he died in 1970, he was buried in Arlington National Cemetery.

Q. What was the last year that trolley cars operated in Butte?
A. 1937. The Butte City Street Railway Company put the first streetcar into operation on Butte Hill in 1886. The first trolleys were drawn by horses. In 1887 many were powered by steam. The system was converted to run on electricity in 1890.

Q. When did pork chop sandwiches go on sale on the corner of Mercury and Main Streets?
A. John Burklund began selling them out of a wagon there in 1924.

Q. When did John open a restaurant in the same spot?
A. In 1932, he opened a space at 8 W. Mercury Street with a counter, 10 stools and a walk-up window.

Q. What is the space like today?
A. Although Pork Chop John's (www.porkchopjohns.com) has opened a second store in Butte and another in Bozeman, and ships its pork chop patties around the country, the original stove still has a counter, 10 stools and a walk-up window.

Q. Elmer Johnson worked as a messenger and delivery boy out of the Thornton Hotel in the 1910s and 1920s. Known by his nickname Lemons for his childhood love of citrus, how many meals and messages did he deliver over his 25-year career?
A. 100,000.

Q. What was Elmer Johnson's distinctive shuffling walk called as he balanced trays on his head to deliver meals?
A. Lemons' Stride.

Q. Who was Lemons' most famous customer?
A. When Charles A. Lindbergh flew into Butte and stayed at the Finlen Hotel in 1927, Lemons delivered his breakfast.

Q. What did Charles A. Lindbergh share with Lemons?
A. A bottle of milk. Lemons accepted the offer and told him "Partner, you're the only man in the world I'd drink this stuff with."

Q. Which Butte mine was the first underground mine in the world to use detachable drill bits?
A. The Anaconda Mine in 1928.

Q. Where did FBI director J. Edgar Hoover banish agents to if they got on his bad side?
A. Butte. It was cold but they soon learned that the trout fishing was pretty good in the summer and it secretly became known among agents as a plum assignment.

Q. When did Butte receive natural gas service?
A. September 1931.

Q. What Butte person had a hand in establishing the International Peace Park in 1932 that joins Waterton Lakes National Park in Canada and Glacier National Park in the United States?
A. Thomas Jefferson Davis was a member of the first Rotary Club in Montana (in Butte) and became the president of Rotary International. He is memorialized on a plaque on the west side of the Peace Park Memorial.

Q. Where was the birthplace of the U.S. Congressman who represented Montana in Congress from 1939 to 1941?
A. Jacob Thorkelson was born in Egersund, Norway, on September 24, 1876. He was a doctor and a surgeon in Butte before and after serving in the 76th Congress. He died in Butte and is buried in Holy Cross Cemetery.

Q. How long did the longest strike in Butte's history last?
A. The longest strike in Butte's history lasted eight and a half months from July 15, 1967, to March 30, 1968.

Q. How did Salvador Allende, President of Chile from 1970 to 1973, save Butte's historic Uptown district?
A. A program called Butte Forward was organizing efforts to relocate the city to the valley so mining could take place where the buildings stand in Uptown Butte. When Salvador Allende was elected in Chile in 1970, he nationalized the copper properties of the Anaconda Company at Chuquicamata, Chile, and crippled the corporation which was sold shortly afterwards to Atlantic Richfield Company at a fire sale price. The expansion of the Berkeley Pit, which would have doomed uptown Butte, was abandoned.

Q. What percent of the Anaconda Copper Company's profits came from their mines in Chile?
A. Two thirds of the corporation's total profits.

Q. Why did the oil company Atlantic Richfield Co. want to buy a copper mine?
A. One theory is that the oil company had astronomical windfall profits from oil development in Alaska and needed to show a substantial loss to avoid a huge tax liability. The Anaconda Company was a good investment to show a loss to their bottom line.

Q. How far apart were Alexy Semonov and Liza Alekeyeva when they exchanged their wedding vows in Butte in June 1981?
A. At the time of their proxy wedding, Liza was in Moscow, Russia, and Alexy was in Butte (5,192 miles or 8356 kilometers apart). Semonov took advantage of the legality of proxy marriages in Montana to marry her there because she was not allowed to leave the Soviet Union. The proxy wedding made international headlines because Alexy was the stepson of Russian nuclear scientist dissident Andrei Sakharov.

Q. If Liza Alekeyeva could not attend the wedding, who stood in her place?
A. A bald friend named Ed Kline held Semonov's hand during the proxy ceremony at the Butte-Silver Bow Courthouse.

Q. When did the last brothel close in Butte's red light district?
A. The Dumas Brothel was closed down as a working bordello in 1982 after 92 years in business.

Q. In the 1995 documentary *The Irish in America: The Long Journey Home*, the Irish immigrant experience is described for what American cities?
A. Boston, Chicago, New York, and Butte.

Q. What were the revenues of Montana Power Co. in 1993?
A. Approximately $1 billion dollars for the statewide utility company headquartered in Butte. Founded in 1912 to feed power to the mines, Montana Power was the state's only Fortune 500 company.

Q. After deciding to invest in fiber optics and establish a telecommunications company called Touch America in 1983, what are the revenues of Montana Power Company today?
A. $0. The Montana Power Company no longer exists. As reported by Steve Kroft of *60 Minutes* in February 2002, in 1997 the utility industry was deregulated in Montana. Soon after, the Montana Power Company sold all of its generating assets and invested the proceeds in their telecommunications subsidiary Touch America. The company's plan was to take the $2.7 billion dollars from the sale of Montana Power's assets and lay a 26,000-mile fiber optic network that would carry voice video and data transmission across a dozen western states. It was the brainchild of Montana Power/Touch America CEO Bob Gannon of Butte.

Q. What was the severance package for Bob Gannon who attempted to turn a stock that sold for $30 a share into one that sold for $100 a share and instead ended up with one that disappeared at less than $.33 a share?
A. Butte born and raised Bob Gannon, CEO of Montana Power and then Touch America, received a severance package worth $140 million before both companies disappeared.

Q. Where in Butte can you find license plates from every U.S. state and Canadian province?
A. The Piccadilly Museum of Transportation Memorabilia (www.piccadillymuseum.com) contains a huge collection of license plates, subway signs, cars and all things related to transportation in their Butte museum thanks to international collector and promoter Jeff Francis.

Q. What was a "Duggan?"
A. Slabs of unstable rock in underground mines were known as "Duggans," after the most popular local funeral parlor. New workers were handed a tool to pry loose the slabs with the order to go "Bar down them Duggans." They frequently fell, killing the miner, who would be taken to Duggan's Funeral Parlour.

Q. What was a nipper?
A. The mine worker assigned to fetch tools as needed and to keep tools in good working shape.

Q. What was a honey car?
A. An ore car in the underground mines that was converted with a seat for the comfort of miners as a mobile restroom.

Q. How many Roosevelts have visited Butte?
A. Four. President Theodore Roosevelt (1903), Lt. Colonel Theodore Roosevelt (son of the president – 1919), Franklin Delano (1920 and again in 1932) and Eleanor Roosevelt (1937).

Q. How many Kennedys have visited Butte?
A. John and Jackie Kennedy (1959), Robert Kennedy (1966) and Ted Kennedy (1972 and twice campaigning for his brother Jack in 1960).

Q. How many U.S. Presidents have visited Butte?
A. Eleven. Dwight Eisenhower (1952), Gerald Ford (1980), Warren J. Harding (1923) Herbert Hoover (1939), Lyndon B. Johnson (1964) John F. Kennedy (1959), Richard Nixon (1951 and 1954), Franklin Delano Roosevelt (1920 and 1932), Theodore Roosevelt (1903), William Howard Taft (1911), and Harry Truman (1948 and 1950).

Q. Presidents from what other countries have visited Butte?
A. Mary McAleese, The President of Ireland, made a state visit to Butte on May 20, 2006. Before that, Eamon de Valera, who would become the third President of Ireland, visited Butte on August 28, 1919.

ENTERTAINMENT

Q. How many times did Charlie Chaplin perform in Butte?
A. Between October 1910 and December 1913, Charles Chaplin made five major vaudeville tours throughout North America with the Fred Karno Company of English Comedians. He appeared in Butte on April 17, 1911, September 18, 1911, March 18, 1912, December 9, 1912, and August 18, 1913.

Q. Where was Chaplin performing his vaudeville act when he received a telegram from Mack Sennett to come make silent movies in Hollywood?
A. Butte, Montana.

Q. Who was the understudy for Charlie Chaplin when he appeared in Butte?
A. An unknown English comedian named Stanley Jefferson who would later change his stage name to Stan Laurel before teaming up with Oliver Hardy.

Q. Who wrote in his 1964 autobiography that Butte had the most beautiful women in any red light district of the world?
A. Charlie Chaplin wrote "Butte boasted of having the prettiest women of any red-light district in the West, and it was true. If one saw a pretty girl smartly dressed, one could rest assured she was from the red-light quarter, doing her shopping."

Q. What event on the street made a lasting impression about Butte for Chaplin?
A. He witnessed a fat sheriff on the street shooting at the heels of an escaped prisoner until the prisoner was cornered in an alley.

Q. When did famous frontier performer and future and Hollywood star Eddie Foy perform in Butte?

A. Eddie Foy, who went on to Broadway and film fame, played an extended engagement in Butte in 1883 at $75 a week. He worked with his partner Jim Thompson and their wives under contract to Butte promoter John A. Gordon, owner of the Renshaw Hall.

Q. What Butte girl starred in her own national adventure serial, *The Adventures of Kathlyn*?
A. Kathlyn Williams, born in Butte on May 31, 1888.

Q. How many films did Kathlyn Williams make during her film career?
A. 175 silent and talkie films from 1908 to 1935.

Q. In what classic cartoon episode was Butte disguised as Washington, D.C., for devious purposes?
A. Boris Badenov and Natasha Fatale try to trick Bullwinkle the Moose and take over Moosylvania in a 1961 episode of *The Adventures of Rocky and Bullwinkle: The Whistler's Moose*.

Q. When would you have heard: "I got you, Butte?"
A. In 1976, on Show 10 of the first season of the Sonny and Cher Show, reporter Barbara Nauseous (Cher) interviews an aging Snow White (Sherman Hemsley) in a Butte diner to get an update on the seven dwarfs.

Q. According to Don Rosa, when did Scrooge McDuck meet Marcus Daly?
A. In his 1995 comic book classic *The Life and Times of Scrooge McDuck*, Don Rosa dedicates Part 4, *The Raider of the Copper Hill (1883 - 1885)* to Butte lore. In that episode, Scrooge takes some prospecting lessons from Howard Rockerduck and almost takes over the Anaconda Copper Mine in Butte from Marcus Daly.

Q. What city produced the world's most famous female impersonator?
A. Bill Dalton of Butte used the stage name Julian Eltinge (taken from the names of Butte schoolmates) and performed across the country as a woman in many roles in vaudeville, silent and sound films. At the height of his career, Eltinge's personal for-

tune was estimated at more than $250,000 and he entertained Hollywood's top stars at one of the most lavish mansions of the time, Villa Capistrano, where he lived with his mother.

Q. How many times did Julian Eltinge perform in Butte?
A. Julian Eltinge returned to his hometown to perform in 1910, 1912, 1913, and 1919. On January 22, 1910, he appeared as second billing to Harry Lauder. In 1919 at the Broadway Theater he introduced a new song titled "The Cute Little Beaut from Butte, Montana."

Q. Who was the other famous female impersonator from Butte, Montana?
A. Mansel Boyle of Butte reached his height of popularity on the vaudeville stage from 1903 to 1913 performing as "Vardaman the Auburn Haired Beauty." Boyle worked in a Butte liquor store until he performed as a woman in a local theater group called The Overland Minstrels. He soon quit his job and left for New York, eventually performing throughout the country in vaudeville theaters. He eventually operated the Eltinge Theater in New York City on 42nd Street.

Q. What King of Hollywood was stranded in Butte and had to bum a meal and hop a freight train from Butte?
A. Clark Gable came to Butte from Kansas City with a traveling troupe called The Jewell Players in 1922. After two months on the road, the group folded in Butte and the stranded Gable had to hop a freight train to Portland, Oregon.

Q. What movie actor is seen driving a car to Butte, Montana, in two different movies?
A. Tim Roth in *Bodies, Rest and Motion* (1993) and again in *Don't Come Knocking* (2006).

Q. Why is Roth's character driving toward Butte in *Bodies, Rest and Motion*?
A. Roth plays Nick, a recently unemployed TV salesman who decides to move to Butte, Montana, because he read somewhere that Butte is "the city of the future." In the film he deadpans "I read that a while ago, so the future should be there by now."

Q. What famous playwright and actor filmed a scene where he sits on a couch on a Butte street all night?
A. Sam Shepherd in *Don't Come Knocking* (2006).

Q. Who is the biggest butt from Butte, Montana?
A. Martin Short as *Jiminy Glick in Lalawood* (1994). Comedian Martin Short created the latex-lathered character who is a local TV entertainment critic from Butte, Montana. When Glick arrives at the Toronto Film Festival determined to make his mark as an interviewer, his dreams are realized when he is granted an exclusive interview with an elusive young star. Soon after everyone wants to be interviewed by Jiminy Glick, including an aging Hollywood actress who is soon found dead in his bed, entangling him in an unraveling whodunit with sex, scandal, rappers and glamorous celebrities along the way.

Q. What brought Jon Voigt and Lou Gossett, Jr. to Butte in 1992?
A. *Return to Lonesome Dove*, filmed in the Butte area that year.

Q. What did Lenny Bruce say about being Jewish in Butte?
A. Leonard Alfred Schneider (Lenny Bruce) was born in New York City and once said of Butte: "To me, if you live in New York or any other big city, you are Jewish," he once said. "It doesn't matter even if you're Catholic; if you live in New York you're Jewish. If you live in Butte, Montana, you are going to be goyish if you're Jewish."

Q. After coming to Butte to film *The Killer Inside Me* in 1974, where was Stacy Keach's lost wristwatch found?
A. Ruby Garrett, the madam of The Dumas Brothel, found it after he visited the establishment.

Q. When was Butte's first St. Patrick's Day parade held?
A. March 17, 1882.

Q. Why did St. Patrick's Day parades stop in Butte for decades?
A. As with many public celebrations in Butte, too often they were a good warm up for a riot, most notably in 1918 and 1922.

Q. What country was represented by the flag carried in the first modern St. Patrick's Day parade in 1981?
A. Mexico. A Mexican flag was handy and an Irish flag was not.

Q. How long has Butte been celebrating the 4th of July with a parade?
A. Since July 4, 1878.

Q. Does Butte set off fireworks on the 4th of July?
A. No. Butte's spectacular Independence Day fireworks display erupts from above the M on Big Butte every year on the evening of July 3rd.

Q. What did actress Martha Raye have to do with Butte, Montana?
A. She was born Margaret Teresa Yvonne Reed at a vaudeville theatre in Butte on August 27, 1916. A patriot who performed for combat troops throughout her life, she was buried with full military honors at Fort Bragg, North Carolina, on October 19, 1994.

Q. What Oscar-nominated actress read for the role of Melanie in *Gone with the Wind* but lost out to Olivia deHavilland?
A. Andrea Leeds, born Antoinette Lees in Butte, Montana, on August 14, 1914.

Q. Who was the bartender on *Gunsmoke* from 1956 to 1959?
A. Bert Rumsey, who played Sam the Bartender on *Gunsmoke* for three seasons, was born Burtis Harwood Rumsey in Butte on October 15, 1892.

Q. What famous redhead pretended to be from Butte, Montana, most of her life?
A. Lucille Ball, who was born in Jamestown, NY, said that she probably knew more about Butte because she often pretended to be from there to seem more like a person from America's heartland.

Q. What famous actor once owned a minor league baseball team in Butte?
A. Golden Globe-winning actor Bill Murray (*Broken Flowers,*

Groundhog Day, Ghostbusters) once owned the Butte Copper Kings with partner Mike Veeck. He came to Butte to cheer for the home team in 1998 and became a local legend for stealing the tourist trolley from the Chamber of Commerce and driving it onto the ball field.

Q. What did Jon Stewart's *Daily Show* have to say about the Butte Chamber of Commerce's efforts to turn the Berkeley Pit into a tourist attraction?
A. Correspondent Jason Jones on the June 22, 2006, broadcast of Comedy Central's *The Daily Show* presented his report that told how the city of Butte has taken lemons and turned them into something that if you drink it, it could kill you.

Q. What was the title of Jason Jones' report about the Berkeley Pit from Butte?
A. *Bad Pit*.

Q. What inspired Thomas Schadt to direct a documentary film about Butte, *Die Vergessene Stadt* (The Forgotten City) in 1992?
A. His curiosity about Butte was first piqued by the photo image of the view from the Finlen Hotel in Robert Frank's seminal book of photography published in 1958 titled *The Americans*.

Q. Who was the headliner at the first ever Bangkok Jazz Festival, performing some of His Majesty, The King of Thailand's original compositions?
A. Actress and jazz singer Eden Atwood who was raised in Butte. Eden is the result of a marriage between Hub Atwood, a writer and arranger for, among others, Frank Sinatra, Harry James, Stan Kenton and Nat King Cole, and her mother, Helen "Gus" Miller.

Q. What was Eden Atwood's maternal grandfather?
A. Gus Miller, the wife of Shag Miller, a Butte radio station owner and personality for many years, is the daughter of Pulitzer-prize winning Montana author A.B. Guthrie, author of *The Big Sky*. Gus Miller has been a guiding force in Butte for the dramatic arts, leading the renaissance of the Mother Lode Theatre. Among many other well-deserved awards for her lifetime of service to the arts in Montana, in 2001 she received the Montana Governor's Humanities Award.

Q. Why is Helen "Gus" Miller in Butte?
A. Love for her husband, a Butte native, originally brought Miller to Butte but her love for the city has kept her connected through the years. She remains involved with arts organizations around Montana but prefers Butte to call home.

Q. Where was *A Thousand Pieces of Gold* filmed?
A. The 1991 movie about Chinese immigrants to the West was filmed throughout Montana including a scene in historical China Alley in Butte.

Q. Where did Hollywood actress Jean Parker, who starred with Katherine Hepburn in the 1933 version of *Little Women*, get her start?
A. She was born Louise Stephanie Zelinska in Butte on August 11, 1905. She changed her name and signed with MGM, making 16 films between 1932 and 1935.

Q. What film by director King Baggot was based on a book set in Butte?
A. *Perch of the Devil*, released in 1927, is based on the 1914 novel of the same title by Gertrude Atherton. The climax of the film is a fight scene between the two female stars Mae Busch and Jane Winton in a flooding mine.

Q. Butte has the state's oldest orchestra. What year was it founded?
A. Butte's Symphony Orchestra was founded in 1951.

Q. Who was the first conductor of the Butte Symphony Orchestra?
A. Anton Leskovar was the first conductor at the first performance on May 4, 1955. Leskovar was a Slovenian who fled Europe at the beginning of World War I. He had performed with the Chicago Symphony Orchestra before coming to Montana and to Butte.

Q. Where is the world's shortest, loudest and coldest Chinese New Year's Parade?
A. Butte's Mai Wah Society has organized the annual parade since 1991 that follows a ceremonial dragon a few blocks to the Mai Wah Museum on West Mercury Street to announce the arrival of the

lunar New Year in January or February, depending on the cycle of the moon.

Q. How many firecrackers and fizgigs are set off after the Butte Chinese New Year's parade?
A. 10,000.

Q. Where did Butte get a Chinese parade dragon?
A. The dragon was made in Taipei, Taiwan, and shipped to Butte in 1988 as a gift to the people of Montana.

Q. What does "*Mene hitteen heinasirkka!*" mean?
A. "Go to hell, grasshopper!" is the traditional cry in Finnish that concludes the crowning of St. Urho every March 16th in Butte.

Q. Who is St. Urho?
A. St. Urho saved the wine grapes in Finland by driving out the grasshoppers, similar to St. Patrick's legendary eradication of snakes from Ireland, or so the legend goes.

Q. What Butte band entertained attendees of two Democratic national conventions?
A. The Boston and Montana Band of Butte, named after the mining company for whom many of its original members worked, performed at the 1896 Democratic national convention in Chicago, Illinois, and the 1900 Democratic national convention in Kansas City, Missouri.

Q. Who received a private serenade by the Boston and Montana band on their way home from the Democratic national convention in Kansas City in 1900?
A. On July 7, 1900, the special train carrying the Boston and Montana band back to Butte stopped off in Lincoln, Nebraska, and awoke William Jennings Bryan at his residence. They wanted to surprise the newly nominated candidate for president so the band decided to visit him in his hometown. Bryan enjoyed the midnight serenade from his porch in his dressing gown and slippers.

Q. When was the Boston and Montana Band formed?
A. December 22, 1887.

Q. Who directed the Boston and Montana Band?
A. Sam H. Treloar led the Boston and Montana band from its inception until his death 64 years later in 1951. The band grew over the years to include 30 members, all employed by Butte mines. When Treloar died, he was the last of the original six members. The band performed at every important event in Butte's history. Along the way  they would win three amateur band championships, play over 1,000 concerts, serenade every troop train leaving Butte during World War I, and perform for presidents and other distinguished guests. After Treloar's death, the band played on, but disbanded a few years later as the public musical tastes and the loss of their leader took their toll.

Q. Who called Butte's Boston and Montana Band "The industrial wonder organization with an unparalleled record?"
A. John Philip Sousa who performed in Butte on October 6, 1907, and November 6, 1919.

Q. What Butte saloon was once rated as one of the best in America?
A. Luigi's in Butte, home of Luigi's World's Largest One Man Band.

Q. How many instruments did Luigi play at once in his World's Largest One-man Band?
A. 24.

Q. Why was Paneek Panisko held in high esteem by the children of Butte?
A. Francis "Paneek" Panisko was renowned for working as a clown before returning to his hometown. In the 1950s and 1960s, Panisko operated a popular arcade at Columbia Gardens called the Paneek Carnival Emporium. He offered fishing and throwing games but the most popular was a shock machine that for a penny would give kids a mild jolt of electricity.

Q. How many vaudeville and motion picture theatres once operated in Butte?
A. As many as 26. To name a few: The Acme, Alcazar, American, Ansonia, Broadway (which became the Montana) Casino, Crystal, Dream, Empire, Empress, Family, Fox, Grand Opera House, Harrison Avenue, Imperial, Liberty, Lyric, Mission, Orpheum, Pavilion, Peoples, Park Grand, Princess, Rialto, Renshaw Hall, and the Theatre Comique, Butte's burlesque stage in the 1880s.

Q. How many of these grand old theatres remain in Butte?
A. One—The Mother Lode Theatre (formerly the Fox on West Park Street).

Q. What famous performer graced the Mother Lode stage recently?
A. Garrison Keillor produced a live performance of *Prairie Home Companion* from the stage of the Mother Lode Theatre which was broadcast nationally on June 5, 1999.

Q. What was one of the highlights of that Prairie Home Companion show?
A. Montana Cowboy poet Paul Zarzyski reading his poem "Why I Like Butte."

Q. When did the Yankee Doodle Dandy perform in Butte?
A. George M. Cohen entertained in Butte on January 1 and 2, 1910.

Q. What internationally acclaimed film director calls Butte his "favorite American city"?
A. Wim Wenders, director of *Don't Come Knocking* (2006).

Q. What is Mesopust and why was it celebrated in Butte?
A. Mesopust is a Croatian pre-Lenten variation on Mardi Gras that came to Montana with Eastern European immigrants who worked in the mines and smelters of Butte, Anaconda, and Great Falls. After a lot of serious singing, dancing, and mock jurisprudence, a stuffed effigy named Mesopust, representing all that went wrong or unfinished in the previous year, is found guilty and burned on Ash Wednesday to make room for good things to arrive in the coming year. The festival is no longer celebrated publicly in Butte.

Q. Why do the Pipes and Drums Band of the Edmonton, Alberta, Police Service come each year to perform at the St. Patrick's Day and Fourth of July Parades in Butte?
A. In May 1983 FBI Agent and Butte resident Gary Lincoln taught an FBI SWAT course to members of the Edmonton Police Service. He invited them to visit Butte. In March 1984 members of the pipe band took him up on the offer and attended the St. Patrick's Day celebrations and performed in various bars. The next year, six members of the pipe band marched in the annual parade. The pipe band has traveled to Butte each St. Patrick's Day since to join the festivities and march in parades.

Q. Who was the head of publicity for MGM Studios until he fell in love with a Butte girl?
A. Henri Verstappen, who moved to Butte in the late 1950s and took a position with the Anaconda Company to be with his wife Peggy.

Q. What is Butte's "coolest" event of the year?
A. The annual ice sculpting contest in December when dozens of sculptures are chipped and carved on the streets of Uptown Butte.

Q. How much does each block of ice weigh when delivered to contestants?
A. 340 pounds.

Q. Why did the Divine Sarah Bernhardt perform at a Butte ice rink instead of a theatre?
A. When Sarah Bernhardt came to Butte on May 5, 1906, she performed at the Holland Ice Rink. Her management was not affiliated with a union, even though she was one of the most famous actresses in the world, so the theaters would not allow her to perform and her appearance was moved to the ice rink at the last minute.

Q. Was she cramped for room at the rink?
A. The rink was modified to seat an audience of 6,000. Admission was $3 per person for the best seats. Bernhardt at age 61 was on her last transcontinental U.S. tour and performed *Camille*.

Q. Where can some of Butte's older residents remember seeing Rudolph Valentino dance in Butte?
A. Rudolph Valentino came to Butte on May 28, 1923, to judge a beauty and dance contest at the Columbia Gardens as part of a national tour sponsored by the cosmetics company Mineralava. A highlight of his Butte visit was an exhibition where he danced the Argentine Tango with his second wife Natacha Rambova, a former ballerina.

Q. Who was John Maguire, theatre impresario, responsible for bringing to Butte?
A. Maguire brought many of the most notable performers of the day to Butte and he also brought artist Edgar S. Paxson to Butte from Deer Lodge. When Paxson first moved to Butte he worked for Maguire as a set painter.

Q. Will Rogers never met a man he didn't like. Did he meet any from Butte?
A. Will Rogers appeared in Butte three times. He performed on the vaudeville circuit at the Majestic Theater on March 12, 1907. He returned for a week at the Orpheum Theater in Butte starting on February 27, 1909. He was advertised as part of a show that featured him as an expert lariat thrower. On his third visit, Rogers returned as a major star on March 29, 1927, flying into Butte and getting a guided tour of the Leonard Mine to the 2,000 foot level before his performance.

Q. What was the first motion picture to be projected in Butte?
A. A film of the fight in Carson City, Nevada, between world heavyweight champion James J. "Gentleman Jim" Corbett and Robert L. "Ruby Bob" Fitzsimmons on March 17, 1897, was shown in 1899 at the Maguire Opera House thanks to Butte banker James Murray who secured the film to show his Butte friends.

Q. Where did Al Jolson begin his solo career?
A. Al was a hit when he opened as a solo act in Butte, Montana, as a 'singing comedian.' One biographer claims he wore white socks, a dark ill-fitting suit with a red bow tie, brown gloves, and a jagged-brimmed straw hat that sat on top of his head.

Q. Did Al Jolson ever return to perform for Butte audiences?
A. Jolson returned to headline in Butte theaters several times. For example he appeared at the Broadway Theater on August 30, 1915, as the star of *Dancing Around*.

Q. When did Butte first appear on the radio waves?
A. Butte broadcasting pioneer E. B. Craney founded Butte's first radio station KGIR which went on the air on January 31, 1929, in the Shiner's Furniture Building on East Park Street.

Q. When did Butte get a TV station?
A. Again thanks to E.B. Craney, Butte received a television station, KXLF-TV in 1953, the first in Montana that still broadcasts as the CBS affiliate throughout Southwest Montana.

Q. Who was the itinerant thespian that brought drama and then theatres to the booming mining camp that would become Butte?
A. John Maguire came to the mining camp that would become Butte City from Salt Lake in 1875. He was an instant hit with his dramatic readings of *Over the Hill to the Poorhouse* and *Shamus O'Brien*. He liked the camp and returned each year. In 1880 he opened Owsley's Hall, and in 1885 he expanded to open the Maguire Opera House on West Broadway.

Q. Who was every vaudevillian's favorite uncle in Butte in the late 1890s?
A. Richard Perry Sutton was known to everyone as "Uncle Dick" Sutton. The performer first came to Butte in 1892 with a traveling troupe performing *Uncle Tom's Cabin*. He would stay in Butte and eventually build four theatres, including the famous Broadway Theater on West Broadway. Uncle Dick was a friend to every performer who passed through the Northwest and was responsible for booking much of the world-class talent that graced Butte's stages during his time. When he died in California in 1924, his remains were returned for interment in Butte's Mountain View cemetery at his request.

Q. What was the name of the theater Uncle Dick built?
A. He built a grand theater that he first named The Sutton. He renamed the theater the Broadway in 1915 and the name changed again to the Montana Theater in the 1930s. The stage was large enough to handle full-scale Broadway productions with full orchestras.

Q. How many seats did the Broadway Theater hold?
A. 2,282.

Q. Was actress Gertrude Sutton Uncle Dick's daughter?
A. No. Gertrude Sutton was born in Butte on September 1, 1903, and grew up to become a Hollywood actress who appeared in more than 50 films in the 1920s through 1940s. Her father's name was Frank Arthur Sutton from Brooklyn, New York. Uncle Dick did have a daughter but her name was Lulu and he named one of his Butte theaters after her.

Q. What did world-famous Scottish singer and vaudeville comedian Harry Lauder write about his 1919 performance in Butte?
A. Sir Harry Lauder wrote in his memoir *Between You and Me*: "I was in Butte during the war—after America had come in. 'Deed, and it was just before the Huns made their last bid, and thought to break the British line. Ye mind yon days in the spring of 1918? Anxious days, sad days. And in the war we all were fighting, copper counted for nigh as much as men. The miners there in Butte were fighting the Hun as surely as if they'd been at Cantigny or Chateau-Thierry. Never had there been such pay in Butte as in yon time. I sang at a great theatre one of the greatest in all the western country. It was crowded at every performance. The folk sat on the stage, so deep packed, so close together, there was scarce room for my walk around."

Q. How many times did Harry Lauder perform in Butte?
A. He performed in Butte on January 22, 1910, and again as Sir Harry Lauder on December 13, 1919, after being knighted for his patriotic contributions to raise funds during World War I.

Q. During the silent film era where did the soundtrack come from in Butte theaters?

A. During the 1920s Butte silent film theatres employed up to 50 musicians to provide the accompaniment for silent films. All theatres were outfitted with a music pit for at least a solo pianist; the American and Rialto also had pipe organs and nine-piece orchestras.

Q. Where did America's favorite flying cowboy come from?

A. The introduction to the popular 1950s TV show claimed, "Out of the clear blue of the western sky comes Sky King," but Kirby Grant, the actor who played the airborne detective, was born Kirby Grant Hoon, Jr. in Butte on November 24, 1911. Grant was introduced to acting through his training in music. His skill as a violinist in Butte won him a scholarship to the American Conservatory of Music in Chicago.

Q. What was one of Grant's first jobs after he graduated?
A. One of his first jobs was to help make recordings for stars like Bing Crosby. Bing did not read music well so Paramount Studios hired Grant to learn the songs, record them with the studio orchestra and then teach the songs to Crosby. The film was *Pennies from Heaven*.

Q. Why didn't W.C. Fields open a bank account in Butte?
A. During his vaudeville days, W.C. Fields performed his world-famous juggling and pool table routines in Butte. The legend goes that Fields had a mortal dread of being beaten and robbed and that he opened a bank account in every town he performed in under a different phony name. He reputedly had more than 600 accounts in banks around the world. However, when he settled in California, an assistant helped him to consolidate his accounts and they found only 24 bank accounts, all in his own name. When he died on Christmas Day in 1946, he had $750,000 in cash and bonds.

Q. When did Fred Astaire trip the light fantastic in Butte?
A. Along with his sister Adele, Fred Astaire worked the vaudeville circuit and was booked to dance in Butte on January 3, 1909.

Q. Who brought the biggest names in vaudeville to Butte?
A. Butte had an Empress Theater, part of the Sullivan and Considine theater chain which booked acts across the country. Seattle impresario John Considine allied himself with a New York promoter Tim Sullivan in 1906, and by 1911 the Sullivan-Considine Circuit had become the first transcontinental vaudeville chain in America and could offer performers

seventy weeks of continuous work. Considine and Sullivan sold out to Marcus Loew and a Chicago syndicate in 1914.

Q. What was one of Butte's earliest entertainments?
A. The first hurdy-gurdy hall in Butte was opened in 1878. Named after a European instrument, the hurdy-gurdy, a stringed instrument in which the strings are rubbed by a rosined wheel instead of a bow, the instrument became associated with cheap dance halls and women of ill repute who played them. Some of Butte's oldest buildings such as the Curtis Music Hall and the Hamilton Block were built as hurdy-gurdy dance halls for the entertainment of single miners in the mining camp.

Q. How many Butte folks turned out to watch Buffalo Bill Cody's Wild West Show?
A. Buffalo Bill Cody and his Wild West Show came to Butte on September 12, 1908, and performed at the circus grounds on the Flats to the delight of an audience of more than 20,000.

Q. Did any members of the famous Barrymore acting family grace Butte stages?
A. Yes. John Drew of the famous Drew and Barrymore clans performed in *Jack Straw* to rave reviews in Butte on July 10, 1909, at the Broadway Theater. Drew's niece, Ethel Barrymore, appeared at the Empire Theater in *The Nightingale* on May 31, 1915, and then, more than 22 years after John Drew was there, she returned to perform on the same stage at the Broadway Theater to equally enthusiastic reviews in *The School for Scandal* on September 21, 1931. Ethel's grand niece is the Hollywood star Drew Barrymore (named for John Drew) who has an open invitation to visit Butte any time she likes.

Q. How much did it cost to see Miss Billie Burke at the Broadway Theater on May 18, 1915?
A. Seats sold for 50 cents to $2.00 a seat to see the Broadway star, who had recently wed Florenz Ziegfeld, Jr., perform in *Jerry*. Many of the next generation remember her best in her role as Glenda, the Good Witch of the North, in *The Wizard of Oz*.

Q. What was so entertaining about the outside of the Finlen Hotel on East Broadway in 1938?
A. A large crowd gathered at the intersection of East Broadway and Wyoming to watch a human fly successfully scale the outside of the nine-story Finlen Hotel.

Q. Why was a large crowd gathered outside the Finlen Hotel in August 2002?
A. As part of Evel Knievel Week in 2002, a crowd gathered to watch Spanky Spangler set himself on fire and jump out of a ninth-floor window. A professional stuntman, Spangler landed safely on an inflated bladder in the intersection below.

Q. Has Spanky Spangler returned to Butte since then?
A. Yes. In 2003, Spanky crashed a car (on purpose in front of a crowd of thousands) and in 2004 he dived from a 150-foot crane during Evel Knievel Days.

Q. When did Fanny Brice visit Butte?
A. Fanny Brice, the original Funny Girl of Broadway, appeared in Butte in March 1932.

Q. When did a Butte audience get to hear Satchmo swing?
A. Louis Armstrong performed in Butte on June 6 and 7, 1951.

Q. What world famous ballerina performed in Butte?
A. In 1915, grand ballerina Anna Pavlova appeared at the Broadway Theater in Butte along with 80 dancers and a complete orchestra from the Imperial Russian Ballet.

Q. How many lions came to Butte with the circus in 1915?
A. The Al G. Barnes Big 3-Ring Circus arrived in Butte for two days of performances in June 1915. Each day began with a

parade, and the shows that followed at 2 pm and 8 pm featured 600 animals with 65 acts and features including 24 African lions.

Q. How long was the parade when the circus returned to Butte in 1917?

A. The Al G. Barnes Circus returned in July 1917 advertising a parade a mile long, with 1,000 educated animals and 30 lions. That year they had company following soon after with the Carl Hagenbeck-Wallace Circus who came later in July. That circus featured 50

clowns, three trains with 22 tents, eight bands, 400 perform-ers, 60 riders, 60 aerialists, 500 horses, 200 acts, three herds of elephants and 400 wild animals.

Q. Didn't the Ringling Brothers Circus come to Butte?

A. Yes. Between 1884 and 1918, the Ringling Brothers appeared in Butte in 1900, 1902, 1907, 1909, and 1913.

Q. What about Barnum and Bailey?

A. Yes. Between 1888 and 1918, the Barnum & Bailey show came to Butte in 1905, 1910, 1912, 1914, 1916 and 1918. After the formation of the Ringling Brothers and Barnum & Bailey Circus in 1919, the circus came to Butte in 1925, 1939, 1948, 1949, 1953 and 1955.

Q. What inspired the common catch phrase: "Who do you think you are, Barney Oldfield?"

A. This question, which was asked of anyone driving recklessly, was inspired by Barney Oldfield, the first man in America to drive an automobile faster than 60 miles an hour. In 1910 he set a record at 131.25 miles an hour at Daytona Beach, Florida. He toured the country giving demonstrations of his need for speed and appeared in Butte on July 15, 1915, billed as The Famous Automobile Speed King, racing with an aviator named DeLloyd Thomson flying above him.

Q. How much did Barney Oldfield charge for an appearance in 1915?
A. The Butte Elks Club paid Oldfield $4,000 to appear in Butte at the summer exhibition.

Q. What was the entertainment for the Fourth of July Parade in Butte in 1916?
A. That year 30,000 Elks converged on Butte for their annual convention, sponsoring an "animated musical flag" that was composed of 1,200 children in red, white, and blue costumes singing "America the Beautiful" and "The Star-Spangled Banner" as Independence Day parade floats filed by.

Q. When did a Butte audience get to witness a horse perform that was smarter than most of them?
A. Indeed one of the biggest hits of the Passing of West Pageant in 1916 was Lucile Mulhall and her High School Horse that entertained large crowds with displays of dancing skill and intelligence. Equally entertaining were the diving girls on horseback at the same event.

Q. How much did it cost to see Svengali perform in Butte in 1914?
A. Svengali, the Master Mind of Mystery, appeared at Loew's Empress Theater in Butte for the week of October 10-16, 1914, offering two evening shows and a matinee to present a Marvelous Demonstration of Thought Transference for anyone willing to pay the 10 cents or 15 cents for a seat.

Q. In how many Butte 4th of July Parades could you see Tony "The Trader" Canonica?
A. Tony The Trader loved parades and walked or rode in 57 4th of July Parades from 1935 through 1992. Tony got his nickname for having an antique store that accumulated odd and unique items but his biggest claim to fame was in his role as Butte's goodwill ambassador in parades. In 1982, he was honored as the Grand Marshall of the Independence Day celebration in Butte.

ARTS &
LITERATURE

Q. Where is Jack Kerouac's ideal bar?
A. The M&M Cigar Store in Butte, Montana. In a posthumous March, 1970, article for *Esquire* magazine, Jack Kerouac described a visit by bus to Butte the year before: "It was Sunday night, I had hoped the saloons would stay open long enough for me to see them. They never even closed. In a great old-time saloon I had a giant beer. On the wall was a big electric signboard flashing gambling numbers ...What characters in there: old prospectors, gamblers, whores, miners, Indians, cowboys, tobacco-chewing businessmen! Groups of sullen Indians drank rotgut in the john. Hundreds of men played cards in an atmosphere of smoke and spittoons. It was the end of my quest for an ideal bar..."

Q. What American author and lecturer was amazed to find a cosmopolitan audience in the remote mining camp of Butte when he spoke there on August 1, 1895?
A. Mark Twain, who lectured in Great Falls, Helena, Butte, Anaconda and Missoula on his Following the Equator around-the-world speaking tour.

Q. What American detective writer formed his opinions about crime, corruption and the role of the private eye based on his encounters in Butte, Montana?
A. Dashiell Hammett, who wrote the novel *Red Harvest* based on his impressions of Butte.

Q. What did Hammett call Butte in his fictional account of the city?
A. Poisonville.

Q. Where was Hammett's office in Butte?
A. He didn't have one. Hammett was a 21-year-old Pinkerton agent who came from Spokane to get arrested so he could spy on fellow prisoners in jail.

Q. When did Hammett come to Butte?
A. Hammett worked for the Pinkerton Detective Agency in Butte as a strikebreaker during the summer of 1920. By the fall of 1920 he was admitted to the Cushman Institute in Tacoma, Washington, with recurring symptoms from tuberculosis. There, he would meet his first wife.

Q. Where did Hammett learn so much about the labor unrest in Butte of 1914 to 1917?
A. His first wife, Josephine Dolan from Anaconda, Montana, graduated from St. James Nursing School in Butte from 1914 to 1917 and was a first-hand witness to the labor unrest during those years.

Q. What movie was made from Hammett's *Red Harvest*?
A. The film *Roadhouse Nights* (1930) is directly based on *Red Harvest* by Dashiell Hammett.

Q. What Bruce Willis movie was also based on the plot of *Red Harvest*?
A. *Last Man Standing* (1996). Also, *A Fistful of Dollars* (1964) starring Clint Eastwood, and Akira Kurosawa's *Yojimbo* (1961) starring Toshire Mifune, all have striking similarities to the plot of *Red Harvest*.

Q. Who wrote *Copper Camp: Stories of the World's Greatest Mining Town Butte, Montana* in 1943?
A. Butte native William A. Burke wrote the book based on his childhood memories, imagination, and historical research for the Federal Writer's Project.

Q. What was the title of the 1914 novel by California author Gertrude Atherton that is set in Butte, Montana?
A. *Perch of the Devil* is set in Butte with the backdrop of the War of the Copper Kings where two women fight for the affections of a successful miner. Atherton writes, "But if Butte is the

ugliest city in the United States she knows how to make amends. She is alive to her fingertips."

Q. Where was the famous painting *Custer's Last Stand* painted?
A. In a studio on East Woolman Street in Butte just below the Steward Mine by artist Edgar S. Paxson.

Q. What was one of Paxson's most inspired works of art?
A. At the age of 47 in 1898, Paxson could have comfortably avoided a conflict, but he enlisted to serve in the Spanish-American War. In October 1899, he designed a street-spanning arch so his fellow Montana veterans from Company M (Anaconda), Company G (Butte), Company D (Virginia City) and Company E (Dillon) could parade underneath and receive a hero's welcome home. The arch was capped with a clay sculpture by Paxson of "Peace" and beneath that WELCOME HOME in large letters.

Q. What art action greeted the Elks convention in Butte in 1916?
A. Broadway Theater stage designer Edmund Carns proposed to build an elk of epic proportions on the busy intersection of Broadway and Main Streets for the convention.

Q. How big was the Butte Elk of 1916?
A. The statue stood 62 feet tall and 44 feet long with 24-foot high legs that street cars could easily drive between. Copper in the plaster finish gave the statue a green hue. Purple and white lights shone from the antler tips. Blue lights hung between the antlers. The eyes made from 10-inch, 75-watt nitrogen bulbs were lit each night. Motorists could look up and see the flank branded with the fraternal greeting "Hello Bill" in large white letters.

Q. How much was Edmund Carns paid to build the giant Elk on Broadway?
A. $4,000. Heated debate erupted among the local Elks who were divided over whether to dismantle or make a permanent display of the elk, either on a butte above the city or at the nearby Columbia Gardens amusement park. While Edmund Carns tried to raise the funds needed to move the elk to a permanent site, the statue was dismantled and only photographs remain of its imposing presence on Butte streets.

Q. What Montana pioneer and author became Butte's first head librarian after returning from serving as the U.S. Ambassador to Uruguay and Paraguay from 1894 to 1899?
A. Granville Stuart, author of *Forty Years on the Frontier,* served as Butte's first head librarian from 1905 to 1914.

Q. What Butte resident prohibited James Joyce's novel *Ulysses* from being sent through the U.S. Mail because he believed it was pornographic?
A. Frank C. Walker of Butte who served as the 51st U.S. Postmaster General from 1940 to 1945. Walker also served as the head of the Democratic National Committee from 1943 to 1944.

Q. Who wrote a novel about life in Butte that later was made into a movie in 1938 starring Errol Flynn and Bette Davis?
A. One of Myron Brinig's novels, *The Sisters,* the story of three girls from "Silver Bow," was made into a movie in 1938. Brinig wrote novels during the 1930s and 40s including *Wide Open Town* and *Singermann.* He was raised the son of a Jewish merchant in Butte, a setting he fictionalized in his novels.

Q. How many novels did Myron Brinig publish?
A. 21.

Q. Who wrote *The Chinese in the United States* and *The Growth and Decline of Rocky Mountain Chinatowns?*
A. Rose Hum Lee, the American-born daughter of Chinese immigrants, who grew up in Butte's Chinatown.

Q. Who was the first woman to head a sociology department in the United States?
A. Rose Hum Lee (1904-1964) author in 1955 of *The City: Urbanism and Urbanization in Major World Regions,* described as the epitome of the urban theory for Chicago, became the head of the sociology department at Roosevelt University in Chicago in 1956.

Q. What does Barbara Ehrenreich author of *Nickel and Dimed* and *Bait and Switch* have to do with Butte, Montana?
A. She was born and raised in Butte as Barbara Alexander, daughter

of Ben Alexander, a copper miner who left Butte to study at Carnegie-Mellon University in Pennsylvania. Both books are thoughtful looks at the plight of the American Dream after working low-paying jobs at Wal-Mart and in the lower echelons of the white collar world. In 2007 she published a perceptive examination of the need for public festivals in *Dancing in the Streets*.

Q. What Butte girl wrote a sensational book in 1902 about sleeping with the devil, among others?
A. Mary MacLane in *The Story of Mary MacLane* which sold 100,000 copies in its first month and was lauded by Gertrude Stein and Ernest Hemingway as an important new work.

Q. Who starred in the film version of Mary MacLane's story?
A. Mary MacLane herself. She debuted on the big screen in her own story in her film *Men Who Have Made Love to Me* which appeared at the Rialto Theatre in Butte in 1918. The poster for the movie enticed viewers with "Mary had six lovers—do you know them?" and the local paper predicted that it would draw moviegoers "like a house afire or a dog fight at the corner of Main and Park streets." The movie, like the book, was a national sensation distributed throughout the country and billed as being "backed by the greatest national advertising campaign ever given an individual star."

Q. What Butte millionaire is responsible for the core collection of one of the country's most renowned art museums?
A. William Andrews Clark spent his later years touring Europe and assembling a large collection of art. On his death, Clark's will stipulated that his collection be donated to the Corcoran Museum of Art in Washington, D.C.

Q. What is the dream of Glenn Bodish?
A. Bodish, the Executive Director of the Butte Silver Bow Arts Foundation, plans to return Clark's collection for permanent exhibition in Butte (see www.bsbarts.org).

Q. How many newspapers have been published in Butte?
A. According to researcher John Astle, beginning with *The Butte Miner* in 1876, more than 85 newspapers have circulated

on the streets of Butte at one time or another. Many were published for years, some only a few issues. Seven of the newspapers were published daily.

Q. How many newspapers were published in Butte in 1908?
A. There were 22 periodicals in circulation in Butte in 1908. These included everything from the daily *Anaconda Standard* (published in Anaconda but most of its readers were in Butte) to the *Montana Socialist* to periodicals that catered to ethnic audiences such as *Slavenska Jedinstoo* and *The Italian Weekly*.

Q. When did color comics first appear in a Butte newspaper?
A. Richard F. Outcault's "Yellow Kid" first appeared in New York newspapers in 1896. A four-color comic supplement appeared in the *Anaconda Standard* in 1897.

Q. How did Butte's fortunes influence journalism in the U.S. for decades to come?
A. A major partner of Marcus Daly was George Hearst. Hearst's fortune, based in large part on his stake in the Anaconda mine, passed to his wife Phoebe and his son. That son, William Randolph, took his inheritance and invested it in newspapers *The San Francisco Examiner* and *The New York Morning Journal*.

Q. What future leader of the American Communist Party started his career in Butte as a newspaper publisher?
A. William F. Dunne, editor of the *Butte Daily Bulletin,* moved on to head the American Communist Party.

Q. What memoir of growing up in Butte was written in Paris, France?
A. *Mile High, Mile Deep* by Richard K. O'Malley was written while he was stationed in Paris as the bureau chief for the Associated Press in the 1960s.

Q. Was Kilroy from here?
A. At the annual gridiron dinner for newsmen in Denver in 1946, it was revealed that Richard K. O'Malley's middle name was Kilroy. Combined with the fact that he served as a war correspondent for the Associated Press, he was accused of being the

prolific author of "Kilroy Was Here" graffiti scrawled throughout the European Theater. There is no record that O'Malley of Butte denied being the graffiti artist.

Q. Who described Butte as "the black heart of Montana, feared and distrusted?"
A. Montana journalist, historian, and author Joseph Kinsey Howard described the city in his 1943 book of essays, *Montana: High, Wide, and Handsome.* The tenth chapter is "Boisterous Butte."

Q. How did world-renowned lithographer Joseph Pennell (1857-1926) describe Butte in his essay for his classic book *The Wonders of Work?*
A. "The most pictorial place in America."

Q. What reader at Viking Press in New York City first read *One Flew Over the Cuckoo's Nest?*
A. Butte resident, Helen "Gus" Miller. According to Miller "I remember going to the editors and saying, 'We must publish this book,' as if, at age 23, I knew anything." Her literary credentials are good enough, however. Her father A. B. "Bud" Guthrie wrote *The Big Sky* and several other novels and short stories as well as the screenplay for *Shane* (1953).

Q. What Butte native edited *The Sciences* magazine?
A. Butte native Edwin Dobb, Jr. is a former senior editor and acting editor-in-chief of *The Sciences*, a magazine that has been given numerous National Magazine Awards. He has written about science and environmental issues for *Discover, Audubon, Mother Jones, High Country News, The New York Times Magazine,* and *Harper's,* where he has been a contributing editor since 1998. In 1997, Dobb served as the co-author, with Jack Horner, of *Dinosaur Lives,* which *The New York Times* selected as a notable book of the year and *The Los Angeles Times* picked as a best book of the year.

Q. Where does Ed Dobb live now?
A. In Butte. His current work is a book that is a companion to a documentary film about Butte being made by award-winning director Pam Roberts whose previous work includes *Ishi: The Last Yahi* and *Backbone of the World: The Blackfeet.*

Q. How many contributing editors to *Harper's Magazine* were born in Butte?
A. Two, Edwin Dobb and Barbara Ehrenreich.

Q. Union Station in Washington, D.C. is adorned with statues of Roman legionnaires by famous sculptor Augustus Saint-Gaudens. Where can his work be seen in Montana?
A. The statue of Marcus Daly at the entrance to the Montana Tech campus in Butte was designed by Saint-Gaudens and installed in front of the U.S. Federal Building on North Main Street in 1906. Moved because cars tended to slide into the statue when the steep street became icy, the statue now greets visitors to the campus of Montana Tech at the end of West Park Street.

Q. How much was raised to commission Augustus Saint-Gaudens to execute the statute of Marcus Daly?
A. $25,000, including $6,000 raised from the miners themselves. It was the last work completed by the nationally renowned sculptor before he died.

Q. Who was responsible for the statue of Thomas Francis Meagher that guards the front steps of the Montana Capitol building in Helena?
A. Irish immigrants, mostly from Butte, raised $20,000 to erect a statue to honor Montana's first territorial governor, Civil War hero, and Irish patriot.

Q. Who was the honorary chairman of the Thomas Meagher Memorial Association?
A. Marcus Daly.

Q. What famous Montana sculptor was born and raised in Butte?
A. Rudy Autio, who now lives in Missoula, was born in Butte in 1923. Autio is most famous for his ceramic sculptures (www.rudyautio.com).

Q. What renowned wildlife artist's first commissioned work was to paint the school mascot on the wall of his elementary school in Butte, Montana?
A. John Banovich. One of the world's most renowned wildlife

artists began sketching images of wildlife while growing up in Butte. He sold his first oil painting when he as 10.

Q. What does John Banovich receive for his work these days?
A. $2,800 to $80,000, depending on the size and subject of his oil paintings.

Q. What New York fashion house was founded by the heir to a Butte noodle parlor?
A. Jerry Tam (jerrytam.com), New York fashion designer and owner of Form Studio, is the son of Ding Tam, the owner of the Pekin Noodle Parlor, one of the oldest family owned businesses in Butte.

Q. What Butte author has written two books and numerous essays on the art of trout fishing and fly tying in Montana?
A. George Grant began his writing career in 1967 when he edited the newsletter *River Rat* for Montana Trout Unlimited, writing many of the essays himself. He then published two books: *Master Fly Weaver* in 1971 and *Montana Trout Flies* in 1972. He published a collection of his many newspaper essays titled *Grant's Riffle* in 1997.

Q. What Butte author has written a book about the Big Hole River, its land and its people?
A. Pat Munday of Butte, author of *Montana's Last Best River: The Big Hole & Its People* (2001).

Q. What is *Butte's Big Game*?
A. *Butte's Big Game* (1989) by author Pat Kearney documents the 75-year history of Montana's oldest high school football rivalry between Butte High and Butte Central from 1915 and continuing through today.

Q. How many other books about Butte has Pat Kearney written?
A. Four. *Miracle on the East Ridge* (1990), *Butte's Pride – Columbia Gardens* (1994), *Butte Voices: Mining, Neighborhoods, People* (1998), and *The Copper League* (2003).

Q. What former Butte resident has spent a lot of his life in hot water?
A. Jeff Birkby, who has worked for the Butte-based National Center for Appropriate Technology for more than two decades, is the author of *Touring Montana and Wyoming Hot Springs* (1999) and *Touring Washington and Oregon Hot Springs (Touring Guide)* (2002).

Q. What Montana writer of epistolary novels (novels where plot and characters are revealed through correspondence) honed her craft for several years in Butte?
A. Novelist Diane Smith, author of the award-winning epistolary novel *Letters from Yellowstone* (2000) and *Pictures from an Exhibition* (2002), once lived and worked in Butte.

Q. Who wrote *Butte's Climbing Guide* (2005)?
A. Butte native Dwight Bishop. The definitive guide on where to climb rocks in the Boulder batholith was published posthumously after Bishop died in 2004 during a climbing accident in Grand Teton National Park.

Q. How did growing up in Butte help fantasy novelist Patty Briggs in her career which has produced 10 books so far including *Dragon Bones* and *Dragon Blood*?
A. A Butte native, Briggs explained in an interview with *The Alien Online*: "When I started to write about an ancient, isolated keep populated by tough, wild-eyed northerners, it felt like home."

Q. What Montana artist created a large oil painting of the Berkeley Pit's terraced walls?
A. Kristi Hager, who lived and worked in Butte from 1984 to 1997 before moving to Missoula, created a large work called *Open Pit* that is now held in a private collection.

Q. Where did Hager have her art studio?
A. On the top floor of the 7-story Metals Bank Building, one of the tallest buildings in Butte.

Q. When did Hager come back to Butte?
A. In 2000, she organized an "art action" called the Cool Water Hula on the rim of the Berkeley Pit by the Bell Diamond headframe. Women and men from around the state hula danced to the music of *Cool Water* by the Sons of the Pioneers.

Q. How many dancers were there?
A. 150, all in blue sarongs.

Q. Was syndicated advice columnist Ann Landers from Butte?
A. No, but she was an honorary citizen. When she came to Butte on October 2, 1962, to speak to 600 people at the Columbia Gardens Pavilion, Mayor Vern Griffith gave her a key to the city and made her an honorary citizen.

Q. What 2001 novel by a Butte native focuses on the fires of the 1970s in Butte's uptown business district?
A. *The Fire Season* by Patrick C. Lee (2001)

Q. What Native American poet and artist traces her roots to Butte, Montana?
A. Painter and poet Anita Endrezze is the author of four books of poetry. Her mother and her mother's parents are from Butte. Her father is a Yaqui Indian from northwestern Mexico.

Q. What did Robert J. Corbett create from his 1970 Oldsmobile?
A. He and an artist friend, Rhondaveaux, made an art car, The Mirrormobile, that has been featured in magazines, newspapers and film including a brief appearance in Wim Wenders' *Don't Come Knocking* (1996).

Q. How many mirror pieces were used to create the Mirrormobile?
A. 694.

Q. Where did award-winning filmmaker Travis Wilkerson, director of *Who Killed Cock Robin?* and *An Injury to One*, attend school?
A. Wilkerson grew up in Butte and attended Butte High School.

Q. Who founded the Los Angeles Philharmonic Orchestra?
A. William Andrews Clark, Jr., son of William Andrews Clark, founded the orchestra in 1919 with his father's fortune made from Butte copper.

Q. Who founded the William Andrews Clark Memorial Library in Los Angeles?
A. William Andrews Clark, Jr. collected books throughout his life and established the library in the name of his father from 1924 to 1926. When he died in 1934 the library was donated to the University of California at Los Angeles.

Q. What Butte-born author wrote a novel that *The Virginia Quarterly* called "the best Civil War novel ever written"?

A. Novelist Donald McCaig, who grew up in Butte and now lives in Virginia, is the author of *Jacob's Ladder* (1998). He also published an equally well received novel based in Butte titled *The Butte Polka* (1980).

Q. What did artist and publisher Russell Chatham say of Butte poet Ed Lahey?
A. Of Ed Lahey, Butte born author of *The Blind Horses* (1979) and *Birds of a Feather* (2005) Chatham wrote that he is "the state's finest living poet."

Q. Where is the 1994 mystery *Deadman* by acclaimed detective writer Jon A. Jackson set?
A. Butte.

Q. Has Jon A. Jackson written other novels set in Butte?
A. *Go by Go* is a novel he wrote in 1998 drawn around the events and consequences of the 1917 murder of I.W.W. organizer Frank Little.

Q. What Butte girl was almost single handedly responsible for the rapid rise of artist Andy Warhol in the 1960s?
A. Art collector Emily Hall Tremaine, born in Butte in 1908, bought 15 works by Andy Warhol in one year.

Q. What book recounts a Native American woman's wrenching and riveting tale of growing up as a Native American in Butte?
A. *Stolen Life: The Journey of a Cree Woman* (1998) by Rudy Weibe and Yvonne Johnson. It is co-written by Johnson, a victim of abuse and violence who dropped out of school and was convicted of murder in Canada. The book focuses on the possibility of living a spiritual life despite being surrounded by deprivation and suffering.

Q. What journalist, poet and novelist drew on Butte for his inspiration?
A. Berton Braley (1882-1966) worked for Butte newspapers from 1905 to 1909. His first novel published in 1921, titled *Sheriff of Silver Bow,* was based on his experiences in Butte.

Q. How else did daredevil Evel Knievel crash besides failed jumps?
A. In this misguided venture that went down in flames, Evel Knievel travels to Mexico to prepare for a stunt while really evil villains plot to do in the daredevil so they can use Team Evel's 18-wheeler to smuggle cocaine into the United States. Despite being a box office bust, *Viva Knievel!* (1977) brought Hollywood to Butte and gave Evel a chance to play himself on the screen.

Q. Who played Evel Knievel in the 1971 film *Evel Knievel*?
A. George Hamilton.

Q. How old was Butte cultural treasure John "The Yank" Harrington when he recorded his first CD of Irish tunes, *A Celtic Century,* in 2000?
A. 96. The Yank passed away in 2004 at the age of 100.

Q. Who described Butte as a muddy and violent frontier town in his 1927 autobiography?
A. Eddie Foy in *Clowning Through Life* describes his memories of performing in Butte for nearly a year in 1883. After a busy career as an actor and entertainer on the Western frontier and in vaudeville, Foy became one of the first Hollywood stars of silent films.

Q. What Butte author wrote a book in 1977 about a secret auto museum in France?

A. *The Schlumpf Obsession* was written by Peter Verstappen, son of *The Montana Standard*'s society page editor, Peggy Verstappen, about the secret collection of Bugatti.

Q. Who is John Richen?

A. John Richen is an internationally renowned sculptor of stone and metal who lives in Butte. He has exhibited his works in major shows throughout the country, as well as in Amsterdam and Montreal. His works can be seen displayed at Fountainhead Corporate Park in Tempe, Arizona, Arizona Power in Phoenix, Arizona, and the Mayo Clinic in Scottsdale, Arizona, the Weyerhauser Corporation, the University of Chicago Medical School, and in collections in Saudi Arabia and Switzerland.

Q. What is Richen's latest creation in Butte?

A. In 2006 Richen opened the Dodge Brothers Saloon and Eatery, a restaurant, deli and coffee shop in a historic building that had languished on the brink of demolition for 30 years.

Q. What words did author Mark Twain use in 1907 to describe Senator William Andrews Clark of Montana?

A. "By his example he has so excused and so sweetened corruption that in Montana it no longer has an offensive smell. His history is known to everybody; he is as rotten a human being as can be found anywhere under the flag; he is a shame to the American nation, and no one has helped to send him to the Senate who did not know that his proper place was the penitentiary, with a ball and chain on his legs."

Q. What book released nationally in 2006 researches the Granite Mountain-Speculator fire disaster of 1917 that killed 168 Butte miners?

A. *Fire and Brimstone: The North Butte Mining Disaster of 1917* (2006) was written by Michael Punke who teaches political science at the University of Montana in Missoula.

Q. In what Butte building can you find paintings of topless women on the walls?
A. Actually, they are feminine portraits of ideals—Justice, History, Geography and Philosophy—on the sides of the rotunda in the Butte Silver Bow Courthouse.

Q. What Butte collector befriended Charlie Russell's only protégé, Joe F. De Yong?
A. In the 1940s while working as a salesman for the Montana Leather Co., Richard Flood acquired an interest in western art and began collecting documents from contemporaries of Charlie Russell. Cowboy artist Joe F. De Yong, trained by Charlie Russell himself, became a close personal friend. Later in life, Flood operated art galleries in Jackson, Wyoming, and Idaho Falls, Idaho. His collection of papers and photographs are kept in the Cowboy Hall of Fame's Dickinson Research Center.

Q. What Butte woman has received numerous awards, including the Berkshire Conference of Women Historians' Article Prize and the Stuart L. Bernath Prize for the best book on American diplomacy for her book *Law, Gender, and Injustice: A Legal History of U.S. Women?*
A. Joan Hoff, who also wrote *Nixon Reconsidered* (1994) and *The Cooper's Wife is Missing* (2005) and appears often as a commentator on PBS, is the daughter of a former miner who left the Butte mines during the 1930s. Both of her grandfathers were immigrants who died young, leaving their wives to raise large families. Hoff credits growing up in Butte with instilling a great sense of history. In her words: "Coming from Butte also taught me about religious and ethnic diversity."

Q. What was the title of the book that the former president of Montana State University in Bozeman wrote about Butte?
A. Michael P. Malone wrote *The Battle for Butte: Mining and Politics on the Northern Frontier, 1864-1906* (1981) before assuming the presidency of Montana State University in Bozeman in 1991 which he held until his death in 1999.

Q. Which other books about Butte have been written by MSU faculty?
A. Jerry Calvert, a professor of political science at MSU, wrote *The Gibraltar: Socialism and Labor in Butte, Montana, 1895-*

1920 (1988) and Mary Murphy, an MSU history professor, wrote *Mining Cultures: Men, Women and Leisure in Butte, 1914-41* (1997).

Q. What was Mary Murphy's job in Butte?
A. Before moving to Bozeman she lived and worked in Butte as the director of the Butte Archives from 1987 to 1988.

Q. What other tomes about Butte have emerged from the University of Montana in Missoula?
A. David M. Emmons, a UM history professor wrote a definitive study of the influence of the Emerald Isle on Butte in 1989 titled *The Butte Irish: Class and Ethnicity in an American Mining Town, 1875-1925*, and Earl Ganz, a UM English professor helped bring Butte-born author Myron Brinig's *Wide Open Town* (1931) back into print in 1993 and in 2006 he published *The Taos Truth Game*, an historical novel about the life of Brinig in Taos, New Mexico.

Q. What was the bargain a Butte portrait artist made to paint a portrait of Maria Weasel Head, the Blackfeet wife abandoned by Joe Kipp?
A. Elizabeth Lochrie was a Butte artist who painted Native Americans. When Lochrie asked to paint her portrait, Maria spit on her. Lochrie persisted and begged until Maria agreed if Lochrie would sit on a pile of manure in the sun while she posed in the shade. The study of Maria Weasel Head is one work in a career that spanned decades that included 2,500 large paintings, 3,000 smaller paintings, two illustrated books and several murals.

Q. Elizabeth Lochrie painted many Montana Indians but what tribe was her favorite?
A. While she painted Indians from the Salish, Crow, Bannock and Blackfeet tribes, the Blackfeet people were her favorite. She often lectured about the Blackfeet culture she encountered and the price of her lectures was a donation of clothing and other necessities for needy members of the tribe. She was adopted by the Blackfeet and given the name "Netchitaki" which translates as "Woman alone in her way."

Q. What Butte artist had an Easter egg that she created for the 1986 White House Easter Egg Roll placed in the Smithsonian Institute in Washington, DC?

A. Sallie Bowen is an award-winning watercolor artist who has painted and traveled in China, Greece, Italy, Turkey, France, Wales and Japan. Bowen's work has been included in national juried shows in Louisiana, Pennsylvania, Maryland, Texas, Georgia, and California and her work is part of private collections in Canada, France, Japan, and throughout the U.S.

Q. What French school of architecture of more than a century ago influenced how Butte looks today?
A. The *Beaux Arts* movement promoted design ideas of order and harmony taught at the legendary École des Beaux-Arts in Paris. The Beaux Arts style flourished between 1885 and 1920 in public buildings designed and built throughout Europe. In the United States, many of the nation's most influential architects studied there and applied what they learned in this country. The style was popularized during the 1893 Columbian Exposition in Chicago as well. Butte's grandest buildings such as the Courthouse, The Butte Water Company, and The Butte Silver Bow Club were built during this time and reflect the architectural ideals of the Beaux Arts movement.

Q. Why does Butte have an abundance of stained glass windows?
A. Some residents were wealthy enough to import stained glass from Europe but many of the windows found in Butte buildings were designed and created by the Butte Art Stained Glass Works Company. From 1892 to 1904 William H. Johnson managed the only business in Montana dedicated to manufacturing glass figure work for homes, churches, and public buildings.

Q. Why did author Betty Macdonald visit Butte in 1946?
A. The author of the 1945 national best seller *The Egg and I* was in Butte to autograph her book in Hennessey's Department Store and to revisit her hometown where she lived until she was nine before her family moved to Seattle. *The Egg and I* introduced the characters Ma and Pa Kettle who would be featured in several Hollywood films over the coming years.

Q. What does Chile have in common with Butte, Montana?
A. In 1998 Janet Finn wrote *Tracing the Veins: Of Copper, Culture, and Community from Butte to Chuquicamata,* drawing parallels between the similar experiences of the two copper mining communities of Butte and Chuquicamata, Chile.

Q. What classic 1935 book details the titanic struggle for wealth and power on the Butte Hill at a time when control of the resources in Butte meant control of all of Montana?
A. *The War of the Copper Kings* by Carl B. Glasscock. The classic account of the epic struggle between Marcus Daly, William Andrews Clark and F. Augustus Heinze for wealth was republished in 2002 by Riverbend Publishing of Helena.

Q. Who is the undisputed master artist of pen and ink drawings of Butte buildings, mine yards and landscapes?
A. Martha Ueland Cooney who has a gallery to display her collected drawings on the third floor of the Metals Bank Building on the corner of Park and Main Streets.

Q. What Butte artist was a close friend of Charlie Russell?
A. Edgar Samuel Paxson. Before Paxson moved to Missoula in 1906, Russell would take the train to Butte from Great Falls to visit his friend and fellow artist. At Paxson's death in 1919, Russell wrote, "Paxson was my friend, and today the west that he knew is history that lives in books. His brush told stories that people like to read...I am a painter, too, but Paxson has done some things that I cannot do. He was a pioneer and a pioneer painter."

Q. What's on the menu at Buster Midnight's Café?
A. *Buster Midnight's Café,* a 1997 novel by Sandra Dallas, is set in Butte. It is one of seven novels she has written since first visiting Butte in the 1980s as a reporter for *Business Week* magazine covering hard rock mining.

Q. Why is Heather Barbieri's first novel *Snow in July* set in Butte?
A. Her father, who grew up in Butte, brought her there for summer vacations from their home in Seattle. Of Butte, Barbieri writes "Perhaps any place visited regularly in childhood takes on a mythic quality in one's consciousness. Butte is definitely a place where myth and reality collide. It's also where I was exposed to the art of storytelling. My Doran relatives, Irish to the core, sat around for hours telling tales of the past with me listening attentively."

Q. Are any of the century-old buildings in Butte haunted by ghosts?
A. Ellen Baumler chronicles the best stories about the residue of humanity that is reluctant to pass on in Butte and other Montana locations in her 2002 book *Spirit Tailings*.

Q. When Wim Wenders set out to film Butte for his recent work *Don't Come Knocking* (2006) what artist was most on his mind?
A. According to Wenders: "Many shots in *Don't Come Knocking* owe a lot to the American painter Edward Hopper; Butte calls to mind his art all over the place. In fact, the entire uptown area looks like one giant outdoor studio in which Hopper might have painted his pictures of lonely and isolated figures in empty cityscapes: same brownstone buildings, same big windows, same lampposts, same advertising on the walls, same abandoned train tracks. Even the colors and the light are straight from his canvases—all of which is not without irony; Hopper was an ardent moviegoer who would leave his studio each time he had an attack of what I'd call 'painter's block.' That his paintings in turn provoked me to see them in Butte and evoke them on film is a sort of strange full circle."

Q. What Butte artist painted the fresco mural at the Mission of San Bernardino in California?
A. Loretta Bonfiglio, born and raised in Butte, studied at the Escuela de Bellas Artes, in San Miguel de Allende, Guanajuato, Mexico. She worked as an assistant to David Alfredo Siguieros, renowned Mexican mural painter. She was commissioned by the Historical Society of Southern California to paint the fresco mural at the Mission of San Bernardino in 1947.

Q. Where can you find a room with a view in the groundbreaking book of photography *The Americans* by Swiss born photographer Robert Frank?
A. The classic book of photography *The Americans* contains images from Frank's tour of America in 1955 and 1956. One image from the book is a gritty view from the window of a room in the Finlen Hotel in Butte.

Q. How many rolls of film did Robert Frank take on his 1955-1956 tour of America?
A. 500.

Q. Where is Butteopia?
A. *Butteopia* (2006) is a collection of photography of modern Butte that captures what remains through the artistic filters of Marcy James, Glenn Bodish, Frank Rufalo, Eben Goff, and others. Of *Butteopia*, reviewer Kris King wrote, "Butteopia feels intimate and real; it captures beauty in unexpected places without flinching from the loneliness of decay."

Q. What Butte opinion writer's columns yielded a Pulitzer Prize?
A. Reuben Maury was born in Butte in 1899. He was an attorney in Butte pursuing a writing interest when an opinion piece in H.L. Mencken's *The American Mercury* was noticed and he was hired by *The New York Daily News*. Maury wrote editorials for the *News* for 52 years, winning the Pulitzer Prize in 1941. At one time he was the most widely read editorial writer in America.

Q. Where in Butte can you find a great independent book store with a staff that actually still reads and recommends books to their customers?
A. Books and Books at 206 W. Park Street owned and operated by Jo Antonioli, the patron saint of Butte authors and book buyers alike.

SPORTS &
LEISURE

Q. Where is the hometown of legendary motorcycle daredevil Evel Knievel?
A. Butte Montana, now home to Evel Knievel Days on the last weekend of July (see www.knieveldays.com)

Q. What broadcast received the highest ratings ever for *ABC's Wide World of Sports*?
A. Evel Knievel's last career jump in 1975 of 14 Greyhound buses at King's Island amusement park in Ohio remains *Wide World of Sports'* highest-rated broadcast with a 22.3 rating and 52 percent share. Of Evel Knievel's seven appearances on *Wide World of Sports*, five still rank among the top 20-rated broadcasts in the show's history, earning a rating of 18.0 or better.

Q. How many times did Evel Knievel jump?
A. At least 300 times, according to Knievel.

Q. When was Evel Knievel's first jump?
A. 1965. In Moses Lake, Washington, Evel Knievel jumped over 50 rattlesnakes and two mountain lions in a 90-foot box.

Q. How much time has Knievel spent recuperating from his crashes?
A. The saying goes that when Evel Knievel wasn't looking for action he was tied up in traction. Knievel estimates he spent nearly three years recovering from his injuries that resulted from his death-defying jumps.

Q. How many bones did Evel Knievel break during his career of daredevil motorcycle jumping?
A. At least 35.

Q. How many bones did Evel Knievel break that belonged to someone else?
A. Two. In 1977, Evel Knievel broke the left arm and wrist of Sheldon Saltman with a baseball bat after he wrote a biography that contained what Knievel said were lies about his family. Knievel was sentenced to three years for the assault and served six months in the Los Angeles County Jail.

Q. According to Evel Knievel, what was one of his most harrowing jumps?
A. In the mid-1970s he was playing golf at Rivermont in Alpharetta, Georgia, and on a dare he jumped a huge ledge on the 17th hole. He nailed the landing in his golf cart but then had to survive the wrath of his wife who was an unsuspecting passenger in the jump.

Q. Which cousin of Evel Knievel from Butte served Montana in the U.S. House of Representatives?
A. Honorable Pat Williams, Democrat, U.S. Representative (1979-1997)

Q. What was Evel Knievel's challenge to all comers when he sold motorcycles in Washington state?
A. He offered a $100 discount on a bike to anyone who could beat him arm wrestling.

Q. Is Evel Knievel still alive?
A. Robert Craig Knievel shed his mortal form on November 30, 2007. At his funeral in Butte on December 10th, 2007, Knievel was eulogized by actor Matthew McConaughey and, in the audience, among the thousands who attended, was longtime friend and legendary boxer Smokin' Joe Frazier. For many of his fans around the world, Evel will live forever.

Q. What Olympic speed skater left Butte to become Governor of Montana?
A. Judy (Morstein) Martz, Republican governor from 2001 to 2005 traveled to Innsbruck, Austria, in 1964 on the U.S. Olympic speed skating team.

Q. What Butte area basketball star was electrocuted in Utah before he could fulfill his promise in professional competition?
A. Wayne Estes (see www.wayneestes.com) from Butte's sister city Anaconda set many records playing at Utah State University. First-team All-America (1965), Estes set records as the second-leading scorer in school history with 2,001 points and the fourth-leading rebounder (893). He holds school records for career points per game (26.7), free throws made in a career (469), consecutive 10-point games (64), points in a season (821), points  per game in a season (33.7), points in a game (52), and rebounds in a game (28) among others. He was electrocuted when he made contact with a hanging electrical wire when he and teammates stopped to offer assistance at an automobile accident scene.

Q. At the time of his accidental death, who was his girlfriend?
A. Judy Morstein of Butte who later became Montana's first female Governor, Judy Martz.

Q. How many teams from throughout the country converge on Anaconda each spring to play a tournament in honor of his memory in the Wayne Estes Memorial Basketball Tournament?
A. 116.

Q. Before gloves were required in the ring, what world champion fought in Butte?
A. World champion John L. Sullivan met Fred Robinson on January 14, 1884, in Butte and scored a bare-knuckled technical knockout in the second round.

Q. Before rules changed, how long could prize fights last?
A. As long as one man remained standing. On May 18, 1884, Duncan "Dunc" McDonald fought Peter McCoy in Butte for the middleweight championship of the world. The fight lasted two hours and thirteen minutes. McDonald broke his hand but continued fighting for 31 rounds, losing to McCoy. In professional boxing matches, bouts are limited to 12 rounds to reduce to risk of serious harm to combatants.

Q. Who holds the Montana state record for the 50 Meter Fly as well as several other Butte records for competitive swimming?
A. Emily Munday of Butte set the record of 30.31 for her age class at the Montana Longcourse Championship in 2006.

Q. What Olympic speed skater lived and trained in Butte during her career in which she won one bronze and five gold Olympic medals?
A. Bonnie Blair, who won Olympic bronze and gold in 1988 in Calgary, in 1992 in Albertville, and in 1994 in Lillehamer, Norway.

Q. Who won the World Cup speed skating championship at 5,000 meters in 1986?
A. Dave Silk of Butte, Montana.

Q. Where have Olympian skaters trained to take advantage of the high altitude before the competitions in Calgary, Alberta, and Salt Lake City, Utah?
A. The United States High Altitude Sports Center in Butte. The outdoor skate oval has been selected three times as the site for the World Cup competition for speed skating.

Q. When was greyhound racing introduced in the U.S.?
A. The first greyhound racing track was built by Owen Patrick Smith of Hot Springs, South Dakota, in 1919 in Emeryville, California, using his inanimate hare conveyor.

Q. When did a greyhound race track get built in Butte?
A. 1925. Smith built tracks around the country after finding success in Illinois and Florida. The track built by Smith himself in Butte was one of the first in the country for the new sport.

Q. Who rode the greyhounds as they chased the rabbit around the track?
A. During the 1930s, monkeys in bright suits rode the dogs as jockeys and whipped the dogs with their tails to urge them on.

Q. Who holds the record for the longest kickoff return in Montana football history?
A. Milt Popovich of Butte returned a kickoff for 102 yards against Oregon State in Corvallis, Oregon, on October 31, 1936. Despite the record setting kickoff return for the University of Montana Grizzlies, the Oregon State Beavers won the game with a final score of 14-7.

Q. Had Milt ever done anything like that when he played for Butte High?
A. Yes. In 1933, he returned a kickoff against the Butte Central Maroons for a 93-yard run. That record would stand more than 50 years until it was broken by Steve Markovich of the Butte Central Maroons in 1988 when he ran from the scrimmage line for 95 yards.

Q. What NFL team did Butte native Milt "The Butte Bullet" Popovich play for?
A. The Chicago Cardinals from 1938 to 1942.

Q. Has anyone else from Butte ever played in the NFL?
A. Tim Hauck, born in Butte on December 20, 1966, played a total of 14 NFL seasons, including stints with the New England Patriots, Green Bay Packers, Denver Broncos, Seattle Seahawks, Indianapolis Colts, San Francisco 49ers, and the Philadelphia Eagles, from 1999-2002.

Q. How many African American halfbacks have played for Butte High?
A. One. Ivan Dunn played on the Butte High squad in 1920 and 1921 before going on to play for the Montana School of Mines where he earned an engineering degree before moving to California.

Q. What cyclist from Butte has followed Lance Armstrong's lead in the *Tour de France*?
A. Levi Leipheimer (born October 24, 1973 in Butte) has been a professional cyclist since 1997. His major results to date are first overall in the 2006 Dauphine Librere, first overall in the 2005 Deutschland Tour, third overall in the 2001 Vuelta de Espana, and three top-ten finishes in the Tour de France general classification.

Q. Where in Butte can you see a yellow leader jersey from the 2000 *Tour De France*?
A. The Outdoorsman is a sports store operated by Levi Leipheimer's brother Rob, and the jersey along with other memorabilia are on display in the store.

Q. What Butte swimmer was named the Women's Sports Foundation's 2005 Individual Sportswoman of the Year?
A. Erin Popovich. Erin began swimming competitively in 1998 and won three gold and three silver medals, and broke four world records, at the 2000 Paralympic Games in Sydney, Australia. She was named the Female Athlete of the Month in April 2004 by the United States Olympic Committee. She was also the 2003 Montana Female Swimmer of the Year. In 2005 Erin was nominated for, and won, an ESPY Award for Best Female Athlete with a Disability as well as being named the 2005 Women's Sports Foundation 2005/Individual Sportswoman of the Year. In case you are wondering, she is *not* related to Butte football legend Milt Popovich.

Q. How did Our Lady of the Rockies get on top of the Continental Divide?
A. An 88-foot Sikorsky Skycrane helicopter supplied by the Nevada National Guard airlifted the statue in sections from December 17 to 20, 1985.

Q. How big is the nose of Our Lady of the Rockies?
A. Our Lady of the Rockies has dimensions that rival the Statue of Liberty. Her nose is four feet long, her eyes are two feet wide, and her lips are three feet wide.

Q. How many breweries have helped slake the thirst of Butte beer drinkers?
A. Butte has been home to 34 breweries. Today there are none.

Q. In 1905, how much beer was consumed in Butte?
A. One brewery, the Centennial, advertised that they sold one million glasses of beer a day. At the same time there were four other breweries operating in Butte – the Butte, the Tivoli, the Silver Bow, and the Olympia.

Q. Where was the gambling game of keno "invented?"
A. Keno, the low stakes game played in casinos around the country, was first developed by Frances and Joseph Lyden of Butte. They modified a game called Pok Kop Piu (the White Dove Game) that used Chinese characters and was played by Chinese immigrants in the Crown Cigar Store where they worked. The Lyden brothers changed the Chinese characters to numbers and took the game to Nevada where it became known as Racehorse Keno, then just keno.

Q. How did future U.S. Senator Burton K. Wheeler end up in Butte?
A. On a break from a 1905 train trip to Seattle, Wheeler lost all of his belongings in a poker game. He decided to stay and practice law in Butte. He represented Montana in the U.S. Senate from 1922 to 1946.

Q. Where does the Guinness Book of World Records list as the hometown of the world's fastest gun?
A. Bob Munden, who lives in Butte, is listed in the Guinness Book of World Records (1980, pg. 625) as "the world's fastest gun," drawing and firing a pistol in 0.0175 seconds.

Q. How did sports events rank in popularity to political events in Butte?
A. In its heyday, just about anything could draw a crowd in Butte. When Montana congresswoman Jeanette Rankin arrived by train on August 8, 1917, she was met by a crowd of several thousand. When airplane daredevil Tex Rankin (no relation) came to Butte on July 8, 1939, a crowd of 10,000 passed through the gate while thousands more watched from outside the gate.

Q. Where was the smallest sit-down restaurant in America?
A. The Success Café on East Broadway in Butte seated four until it closed in 1924. For many years Butte was a Democratic stronghold and Democrats joked that the Success Café was where Butte Republicans held their conventions.

Q. Where was the longest bar?
A. The Atlantic Bar in Butte was a city block long with as many as 15 bartenders. On Saturday nights, they were said to serve 12,000 glasses of beer.

Q. Who is Sean O' Farrell?
A. A Sean O'Farrell is a "what." A popular drink after a shift in the mines, it consists of an ounce of whisky with a pint of beer chaser. The whisky was to cut the copper dust from the miner's throat and the beer to slake the thirst from a full shift in a hot box mine.

Q. World heavyweight champion James J. Jeffries knocked out Canadian boxer Jack Munroe in the second round of their championship match in San Francisco on August 26, 1904. Who got to watch them fight nearly a year before that?
A. Munroe and Jeffries fought a four-round exhibition match in Butte on December 19, 1903.

Q. "Young Firpo," aka Guido Bardelli, was knocking out the competition on the fast track to win the world light heavyweight title when his career was curtailed by a car wreck in 1934. Where was he heading when the accident happened?
A. On his way to Butte, Montana, to fight Gorilla Jones.

Q. How did Young Firpo know Butte?
A. He trained there with his long-time trainer Mel Epstein.

Q. What Butte fighter so impressed champion light heavyweight boxer Jack Dillon that he offered to be his manager?
A. Leo Bens, known as the "Butte Wildcat," was a miner and a sparring partner for Dillon when he came to Butte to fight Bob Moha. Dillon was so impressed with the fighting Butte miner that he wanted to sign a contract as manager and tour the country with Bens.

Q. What was Stanley Ketchel's job in Butte, Montana?
A. Stanley Ketchel, possibly the world's greatest middleweight fighter of all time, worked in Butte, Montana, as a bouncer. He also took on all comers in fights at the Empress Theater. He fought his first professional bout in Butte in 1903. In his Montana career, Ketchel went 40-2. In 1908 he beat Jack (Twin) Sullivan to take the world middleweight title. In 1909 he fought Jack Johnson for the heavyweight championship of the world and lost. While training for a rematch on a Missouri farm in 1910 he was murdered by a jealous farmhand.

Q. How many knockouts did Stanley Ketchel have over his boxing career?
A. Ketchel scored 49 knockouts in 64 professional fights.

Q. Who is Naranche Stadium at Butte High School named for?
A. Eso Naranche was an all-star fullback and track star at Butte High and at Montana State University. He was killed in action in North Africa in 1943.

Q. How much was raised at the 1943 Butte High-Butte Central game for war bonds in honor of Eso Naranche?
A. $3,000, which would be equivalent to $34,959.54 today according to www.measuringworth.com.

Q. What famous Butte fly fisherman patented his fly tying techniques in 1939?
A. Big Hole trout fly-tying legend George Grant.

Q. What mine on Butte Hill built handball courts for its Irish workers for recreation between underground shifts?
A. The Mountain Con.

Q. Who has been the state handball champion more times than any other player since records started being kept in 1919?
A. Bill Peoples of Butte won the state handball single's open championship 1971-1978, 1985-1987, 1991-1993 and in 1999, for a total of 14 years.

Q. How many times has the state single's handball champion been from Butte?
A. 37 out of 84 times. Ray Gallant (7 times), Steve Stanisich (8 times), Bill Peoples (14 times), Justin Balkenbush (5 times) Butch Starin (2 times) and Tom Pomroy (once in 1990.)

Q. How many years did the Butte High Bulldogs wrestling team win the Montana state AA championship under Coach Jim Street?
A. 13. From 1980 to 1992, the Butte High School wrestling team under the guidance of legendary coach Jim Street took every state championship. They won again in 1995 under Coach John Metz for a total of 14 state championships in the last 26 years.

Q. When John Metz left coaching to serve as principal, who took his place as wrestling coach at Butte High?
A. Jim Street came out of retirement to lead the team again.

Q. What Butte High wrestler has won the state title for his weight class for all four years of his high school career?
A. Cole Dallaserra posted a record of 140-13 during his four years at Butte High (2002-2006) where he won the state championship each year at four different weight classes. His freshman year he wrestled at 105 pounds with a 34-4 record; his sophomore year he went 29-3 at 119 pounds; as a junior, he managed to go 37-4 at 130 pounds; and then finished his career with a 40-2 mark at 140 pounds. All four of his state championships were won in the highest classification in Montana.

Q. When was the last Montana Alfalfa Days?
A. In August 2003 promoter Tom Hafer organized snowmobile races on a 500-foot alfalfa grass track near Butte that drew racers and their rigs from as far away as Canada and more than 1,000 spectators for the one-time event.

Q. Who set the world speed record for a snowmobile in 1986?
A. Tom Hafer of Butte at the Budweiser International High Altitude Speed Run in Riverton, Wyoming, set the world speed record that year (on snow) at 136.481 miles an hour.

Q. Where can you enter your bed in a race?
A. Each fall on the Butte campus of Montana Tech, students launch various contraptions usually consisting of mattresses and frames welded to bicycle parts in the Annual Bed Races to see who can get down a steep hill the fastest (and with the fewest injuries).

Q. After his fortune was secure, what became the object of Marcus Daly's passions?
A. Raising and running race horses. Daly kept 1,200 horses on his Bitterroot Stock Farm.

Q. What was the name of Marcus Daly's most famous race horse?
A. Tammany. Daly bought his favorite thoroughbred, Tammany, in 1891 for $2,500. In 1893 a rivalry developed between Daly and the owner of an Eastern thoroughbred named Lamplighter. When a race was set, Daly pledged that if Tammany beat Lamplighter, he would build his horse a castle. When Tammany won by 4 lengths, Daly built his "castle" on a hill near Daly's Georgian mansion about a mile east of Hamilton. The luxurious stable was also home to Daly's other famous thoroughbred stallions Hamburg, Inverness, The Pepper, and Ogden.

Q. Why was the Florence Hotel called The Big Ship?
A. Butte-Silver Bow County Sheriff John K. O'Rourke claimed that the amount of alcohol consumed in the famous boarding house for single miners on weekends was enough to float a ship—a big ship.

Q. How many beds were in The Big Ship?
A. In 1919 the Florence Hotel had 300 beds.

Q. What was the most popular entrée on the Big Ship's menu?
A. The most popular item was an oatmeal mush thinned with milk to thin gruel called "stirabout." Hundreds of men a day filled up on two or three bowls and many took it along for lunch in the mines.

Q. Has Butte produced any skiing champions?
A. John Downey of Butte was a member of the U.S. men's cross-country ski team from 1975 to 1978. In 1977, Downey won five of seven races in the Dannon Series in Vermont. One of his wins was over Bill Koch, a 1976 Olympic silver medalist. Downey missed making the 1976 U.S. Olympic team by 77/100ths of a point. Downey finished second at the 1977 Norwegian Birkebeiner event in Holmenkollen, Norway. Later that same year, he was fourth overall in the 15-kilometer event at the United States National Championships.

Q. What did Robert Craig "Evel" Knievel jump in 1957?
A. In that year he competed in and won the Northern Rocky Mountain Ski Association Class A Men's ski jumping championship.

Q. Who were the Butte Buzzies?
A. The Butte Buzzies was a Butte independent football club (1949 to 1951). The semi-pro team played against local and area college teams and other independent clubs from Billings, Anaconda, Denver and Seattle. The highlight season was 1950 when the Buzzies defeated the Lowry Air Force Base club from Denver 14-6 and the Seattle Ramblers 6-0 before 5,500 fans at Naranche Stadium. The team was owned by Charley Judd of the New Deal Bar.

Q. When did Butte get its first baseball team?
A. In 1902, the Butte Miners joined the Pacific Northwest League and won the league title that year.

Q. What was their record?
A. 72 wins and 47 losses.

Q. What was the name of the all-black baseball team that played for Butte?
A. The Butte Colored Giants.

Q. What did Butte have to do with the 2002 Winter Olympics in Salt Lake City, Utah?
A. The torchs used to deliver the Olympic flame from around the world were made by Seacast, Inc., an investment castings foundry in Marysville, Washington, founded by the Robins brothers from Butte, Montana.

Q. Who has collected the most World Series checks in the history of baseball?
A. Frankie Crosetti, who as a player and then a third base coach was part of 17 championship teams with the New York Yankees, played for the Clarks of the Butte Mines League.

Q. What Butte Mines League player ended up in the Baseball Hall of Fame?

A. Earl Averill who played in 1925 for the Anaconda Anodes of the Butte Mines League was the first American League player to hit a home run in his first big league at-bat and played in the first six All-Star games (1933-38). After a stellar career in the majors from 1929 to 1941, he was inducted into the Baseball Hall of Fame in 1975.

Q. What was a double jacking contest?

A. A drilling contest with two-men teams, one to handle the sledgehammer and the other to hold and twist the steel drill bit. Hard rock miners competed for bragging rights and big cash prizes.

Q. Who was the winner of a mucking contest?

A. Muckers were shovelers. The fastest shoveler always won the mucker's contest. On July 26, 1921, for example, the winner was August Maadda of the Original Mine who shoveled a half ton of ore with a winning time of 2:03. Second place was taken by Steve Erakovich of the Travona Mine with a time of 2:05.

Q. Where was mine safety considered a spectator sport?

A. In the Mining City, of course. The Anaconda Company used competitions to train miners in underground first aid and rescue. Mines sponsored their own teams and competed for prizes and cash awards. On Miner's Field Day in July 1918, 33 first aid teams competed at Columbia Gardens in front of 20,000 spectators.

Q. How many public skating rinks were once maintained by Butte's Public Works Department?

A. As recently as 30 years ago, the county flooded and groomed at least 22 rinks for public ice skating during the winter months. Many others were flooded on private property to provide recreational opportunities for Butte kids.

Q. How many rinks are flooded for public skating today?

A. Eight.

Q. What game did Italians immigrants bring to Butte that has its origins in games played in ancient Rome?

A. Bocce is played with one small ball (Pallino) and eight larger balls. Bocce is singular, several are called Bocci—four for each team. The Pallino is thrown first and becomes the target. Then each Bocce is thrown with the goal of placing it as close to the Pallino as possible. A full game of Bocce is a round, and a round is separated into a series of scoring periods called giri (plural) or giro (singular). In each giro, only one team may score points. A point is scored for the team with its Bocce closest to the Pallino, and additional points are earned for each Bocce of the same team that is closer to the Pallino than the closest Bocce of the opposing team. The team that reaches nine points first wins the round. Most amateur bocce players play on lawns, beaches, gravel paths and even on snow.

Q. What game was brought to Butte by miners from Northern England?

A. Quoits is a tossing game similar to horseshoes. In quoits, metal rings are thrown at target pins at either end embedded in soft clay. Early quoits were made from left over metal from mine forges and quoit playing still has a strong connection to mining communities. Fifteen rules governing the game were published in 1881 that set the rules for what is now called The Northern Game and it has remained largely unchanged ever since. The game has the hobs (stakes that the quoits were aimed at) 11 yards apart in 3 feet squares of clay. The first players used an iron quoit which weighed about a pound but regional variations have resulted in heavier quoits and in Northern England quoits measure about 5 1/2 inches in diameter and weigh about 5 1/2 pounds.

Q. When could you first choose between a bottle or a can of pop to drink in Butte?

A. Butte was one of nine cities in the Northwest where pop in a can was introduced in July of 1953.

Q. What flavors of pop were available in a can in 1953?

A. Grape orange, root beer and black cherry. Each can was sold in the color of the flavor it contained.

Q. What sports team once held the national record for most consecutive losses?
A. The Montana School of Mines Orediggers football team lost 44 games over nine years.

Q. When was their record-breaking losing streak broken?
A. November 3, 1962, when they beat the Northern Montana Lights 33 to 7. These days under Head Coach Bob Green they win more football games than they lose.

Q. What was Colonel Buckets' claim to fame?
A. A popular sight at the Marcus Daly racetrack was James "Colonel Buckets" Rutledge. He was renowned for being able to recite the lineage of every winning horse that ever ran on an American racing track.

Q. How many people were watching when the Copper League played at Clark Park in Butte in 1947?
A. Butte Copper League baseball teams played summer games from 1944 to 1960. During the 1947 season 120,503 fans attended games.

Q. What world record was set by a Butte baseball team?
A. In 1906 the Butte Miners did not allow an opposing team to score in 45 consecutive innings, winning five games in a row as shutouts.

Q. How many Montana state football championships have been won by Butte High School's Bulldogs?
A. 31. The Bulldogs rank in the top five nationally for winning state titles.

Q. When was the first year that Butte High won the state football championship?
A. 1903.

Q. What sport was played by squads on the gridiron 10 years before football?
A. Rugby was brought to Butte by European immigrants and became a school sport in Butte before American football.

Q. Who set the 1916 record for the fastest trip to Missoula from Butte?
A. On September 6, 1916, the automobile speed record of 3 hours, 33 minutes and 30 seconds, from Butte to Missoula (119 miles) was set by Herbert Riley, of Perham & Riley, Butte Cadillac agents. Riley bet on himself and won $600. Thousands of dollars were wagered on the race by others. He beat the record set the day before by John Berkin, manager of Butte's Motor Car Distribution Co., 108 E. Broadway, by nine minutes and 30 seconds.

Q. According to Eddie Foy, what was the most popular sport in the mining camp in the summer of 1883?
A. Foot races. In 1883, camp gamblers wagered heavily on the outcome of foot races. One of the best and most popular racers was Foy's actor partner, Jim Thompson.

Q. Do they rodeo in Butte?
A. Despite a rich industrial history, Butte has always been part of Montana and evidence of that is a long-standing rodeo tradition with cowboy competitions that go back as far as 1916. On July 5 and 6, 1916, The Passing of West Pageant thrilled crowds with rodeo events, trick roping and riding and diving girls on horseback. The Butte Vigilante Rodeo continues each summer as a major stop on the summer Montana PRCA rodeo circuit.

Q. What was one of the main attractions at the Helsinki Bar in Finntown?
A. The Finnish wet sauna downstairs until the bar and the sauna closed in 1999.

Q. Who won the marathon waltz contest of 1909?
A. It was a draw. The county attorney called off the December 8 dance contest at Renshaw Hall after 14 hours and 41 minutes. The contest began with 53 couples and ended with three couples still standing on the floor. When a riot threatened to erupt, the three couples were all declared winners and received the same prizes – diamond rings for the ladies and gold watches and fobs for the gentlemen.

Q. Who beat F. Augustus Heinze at his own game in 1902?
A. At the Silver Bow Club in June 1902, F. Augustus Heinze, the "courthouse miner," met William D. Mangam, vice president of the Montana Music Co. in Butte and agent for W. A. Clark, Jr., in a ping-pong match. Charles W. Clark, oldest son of Copper King William Andrews Clark, was the referee. Mangam was known as the best player in the club, and he soundly trounced Heinze in the match. While Heinze was running circles around his opponents in the high stakes game of legal maneuvers, he was easy pickings at the ping pong table, barely able to return a serve.

Q. Where could you find an African American juke joint in Butte during the 1920s?
A. The Silver City Club was the place to hear Louis Armstrong, Duke Ellington, and Ella Fitzgerald perform *in person* in Butte during the 1920s.

Q. What famous blues pianist was born in Butte?
A. Arthur "Montana" Taylor was born in Butte in 1903. His father owned the Silver City Club until the family moved to Chicago in 1910 and then to Indianapolis and Cleveland. Montana Taylor recorded between 1929 and 1946. Although he recorded only seventeen tracks, he is regarded by some as one of the greatest blues piano players of all time.

Q. In Butte's earliest days just about any activity could result in a riot. Almost every summer picnic featured a tug of war to help relieve tensions. When did a tug of war at a summer picnic result in a riot?
A. On August 11, 1912, the Butte Miners' Union picnic at Gregson Hot Springs (now Fairmont between Butte and Anaconda) was attended by 15,000. A tug of war between Butte Irish and Slavic miners quickly escalated into a riot. The special train that brought many of the picnickers and their beer from Butte was used to haul the wounded back to Butte. Two miners died from their wounds when a cowboy shot them. One, Marco Nicovich, died from his wounds on the train to Butte and the other, Yanko Tusivik, died the following day. A third casualty of the picnic was in an unrelated incident when an Irish miner named Shea fell out of an open train car onto his head and was found dead the following day.

Q. What are Greenisms?
A. Bob Green, the head football coach of Montana Tech's Frontier Conference Montana Orediggers, is known far and wide for his colorful speech on news interviews. Such gems, known as "Greenisms," are looked forward to and cherished by fans throughout Southwest Montana. Here are three: "He is tougher than a stucco bath tub." "He's busier than a mosquito in a nudist colony," and "We are working harder than a cat in a fresh litter box."

Q. Have any hockey players from Butte ever gone on to play in the National Hockey League?
A. Yes. Tom O'Toole who played with the Butte Copper Kings in 1975 went on to play with the New England Whalers of the old World Hockey Association, which later became the Hartford Whalers of the National Hockey League.

Q. What was O'Toole's most vivid memory of playing hockey at the Butte Civic Center?
A. Before a game with Billings on Feb. 14, 1976, known ever after as The St. Valentine's Day Massacre in Butte, the team was getting dressed when fighting broke out in the stands. Suddenly O'Toole saw what appeared to be a bundle of four dynamite sticks tossed onto the ice with a lit fuse. "The fuse was going and I was out the door and in the parking lot with my skates on. It ended up it was four pieces of red broom handles tied together."

Q. What was the nickname for the Butte hockey team?
A. According to O'Toole, the Butte Copper Kings hockey team was often called the "Chopper Kings" by their opponents for their predisposition to fight.

Q. What tragic event resulted in Butte's complex of fields that have hosted state soccer tournaments?
A. The Jeremy Bullock Soccer Complex in Butte was born from a horrible schoolyard shooting that took the life of an 11-year-old Butte boy on April 12, 1994. The fields honor his memory as well as bring children from all over the state in friendly non-violent soccer sports contests.

Q. What little league field in Butte has entered the big leagues over the past few years?
A. Scown Field on East Caledonia Street in Butte hosts little league play during the regular season but every summer they host the Western Region Senior (age 15-16) Little League Softball Tournament championship that brings teams from Alaska, California and Oregon to compete.

Q. Where was Butte's first ball field?
A. Most team sports were played on an undeveloped field at the edge of the mining camp until William Andrews Clark decided to improve the situation in 1902. At the new Columbia Gardens a grand ballpark was built that could seat up to 3,000 spectators in the grandstand and open bleachers to watch a variety of sports including boxing, baseball, and horse races.

Q. How big was the Columbia Gardens ball field for baseball games?
A. 285 feet from home plate to the left field wall, 425 feet from home plate to left centerfield wall, 445 feet to dead centerfield, 400 feet to right centerfield, and 275 feet to the wall down the right field line. The park became the home field for the champion Butte Miners.

Q. How did the Columbia Gardens ball field compare in size to other fields in the country?
A. Built in the Bronx, Yankee Stadium opened on April 18, 1923. Original dimensions at Yankee Stadium were 281 ft. (left), 295 ft. (right), and 490 ft. (center). Centerfield became known as "Death Valley" because of its distance from home plate.

Q. With the arrival of the automobile before 1910, what became a favorite winter sport of Butte children?
A. Hookybobbing or carsurfing on icy streets where they would hitch a ride by holding onto the bumper of an automobile and slide behind the car up a hill.

Q. What was the Arcade?
A. During the Depression single unemployed men were invited to the basement of this building at the northwest corner of the intersection of Park and Main next to the M&M Cigar Store to play board games and cards.

Q. Why was the M&M called a cigar store?
A. During the Prohibition years, a cigar store was a euphemism for a drinking and gambling establishment. You could buy a fine Flor de Baltimore cigar but smoking was not the only vice that you could satisfy in these Butte cigar stores.

Q. Was bowling a popular sport in Butte?

A. It still is with two bowling alleys that remain busy with parties and tournaments but bowling has been a popular sport from the city's beginning. The M&M for example, was built in 1890 with a bowling alley in its basement.

Q. Where was the first multi-purpose sports complex built in Montana?
A. The Butte Civic Center completed in 1952 was built at a cost of $1 million to host hockey and other ice sports and basketball. Two days after the center opened it hosted the 1952 Class A state basketball tournament that drew 31,000 fans.

ABOUT THE AUTHOR

Long time Butte resident George Everett has written more than 100 articles, many illustrated with his own photography, for a variety of regional and national publications. Most of his writing has focused on art, business, travel, and history topics in Southwest Montana for magazines and newspapers including *Horizon Air, American History, American Heritage, Conde Nast Traveler, Great Falls Tribune, Highlights for Children, The World of Hibernia, Historic Traveler, Irish America, Montana Magazine, The Chicago Tribune, The Denver Post* and *The Seattle Times*. More of his writing about a variety of topics can be found on his web site www.butteamerica.com and its companion online magazine, *Only in Butte* (www.butteamerica.com/oib.htm).